SEX THEORIES AND THE SHAPING OF TWO MODERNS

MAJOR LITERARY AUTHORS
VOLUME 11

STUDIES IN
MAJOR LITERARY AUTHORS
OUTSTANDING DISSERTATIONS

edited by
William E. Cain
Wellesley College

A ROUTLEDGE SERIES

Other Books in This Series:

1. THE WAYWARD NUN OF AMHERST
Emily Dickinson in the Medieval Women's Visionary Tradition
by Angela Conrad

2. PHILIP ROTH CONSIDERED
The Concentrationary Universe of the American Writer
by Steven Milowitz

3. THE PUSHER AND THE SUFFERER
An Unsentimental Reading of Moby Dick
by Suzanne Stein

4. HENRY JAMES AS A BIOGRAPHER
A Self Among Others
by Willie Tolliver

5. JOYCEAN FRAMES
Film and the Fiction of James Joyce
Thomas Burkdall

6. JOSEPH CONRAD AND THE ART OF SACRIFICE
Andrew Mozina

7. TECHNIQUE AND SENSIBILITY IN THE FICTION AND POETRY OF RAYMOND CARVER
Arthur F. Bethea

8. SHELLEY'S TEXTUAL SEDUCTIONS
Plotting Utopia in the Erotic and Political Works
Samuel Lyndon Gladden

9. "ALL THE WORLD'S A STAGE"
Dramatic Sensibility in Mary Shelley's Novels
Charlene E. Bunnell

10. "THOUGHTS PAINFULLY INTENSE"
Hawthorne and the Invalid Author
James N. Mancall

SEX THEORIES AND THE SHAPING OF TWO MODERNS
Hemingway and H.D.

Deirdre Anne (McVicker) Pettipiece

Taylor & Francis Group
New York   London

Published in 2002 by
Routledge
Taylor & Francis Group
711 Third Avenue
New York, NY 10017

Published in Great Britain by
Routledge
Taylor & Francis Group
2 Park Square, Milton Park,
Abingdon, Oxfordshire OX14 4RN

First issued in paperback 2014

Routledge is an imprint of the Taylor and Francis Group, an informa business

Copyright © 2002 by Routledge.

All rights reserved. No part of this book may be reprinted or reproduced or utilized in any form or by any electronic, mechanical, or other means, now known or hereafter invented, including photocopying and recording, or in any information storage or retrieval system, without written permission from the publishers.

Library of Congress Cataloging-in-Publication Data

Pettipiece, Deirdre Anne, 1961–
  Sex theories and the shaping of two moderns : Hemingway and H.D. / by Deirdre Anne (McVicker) Pettipiece.
    p. cm. — (Studies in major literary authors ; v. 11)
  Includes bibliographical references and index.
  ISBN 0-415-93786-8 (acid-free paper)
  1. Hemingway, Ernest, 1899–1961—Views on sex. 2. H. D. (Hilda Doolittle), 1886–1961—Fictional works. 3. American fiction—20th century—History and criticism. 4. H. D. (Hilda Doolittle), 1886–1961—Views on sex. 5. Hemingway, Ernest, 1899–1961—Characters—Women. 6. H. D. (Hilda Doolittle), 1886–1961—Characters. 7. Ellis, Havelock, 1859–1939—Influence. 8. Darwin, Charles, 1809–1882—Influence. 9. Freud, Sigmund, 1856–1939—Influence. 10. Modernism (Literature)—United States. 11. Women in literature. 12. Sex in literature. I. Title. II. Series.
  PS3515.E37 Z7537 2002
  813'.52093538—dc21
                                                                 2002002521

ISBN 13: 978-0-415-93786-3 (hbk)
ISBN 13: 978-0-415-86684-2 (pbk)

For my father, James.

Contents

ACKNOWLEDGMENTS	*xi*
PREFACE	*xiii*
INTRODUCTION: "Strange Bedfellows"	*xvii*
CHAPTER ONE: The Emergence of Two Moderns	1
CHAPTER TWO: Tending the Gardens of Darwin, Ellis and Freud: The Roots of H.D.'s Sexual Symbols	9
CHAPTER THREE: Matricidal Tendencies: Hemingway's Battle Begins	19
CHAPTER FOUR: Foreigner at Home and Abroad	29
CHAPTER FIVE: Distant Observations	45
CHAPTER SIX: Catherine (Re)Bourne: Erotic Symbolism in *The Garden of Eden*	59
CHAPTER SEVEN: "Nebulous" Personalities	79
CONCLUSION: "The Sea in Being"	93
BIBLIOGRPAHY	97
INDEX	101

Acknowledgments

I owe a debt of gratitude to many people who made available to me the numerous texts from which I cite material. In particular I wish to thank Nicholas Taylor who enabled me to use sections from *Paint it Today* (reprinted courtesy of New York University Press), Robert Bernheim who allowed reprinting of copious sections of Havelock Ellis's *Studies in the Psychology of Sex*, Scarlett Huffman who provided permissions for *Hemingway* (reprinted courtesy of Harvard University Press), and Michael Katakis who graciously allowed reprinting of sections from Hemingway's *The Garden of Eden* (Simon and Schuster).

I would also like to take a moment here to acknowledge the abiding influence and assistance of my mentor, Bert Bender, whose faith in my ability has never wavered. I would also like to personally and permanently acknowledge my editor, Damian Treffs, whose patience knows no bounds and whose persistent optimism made things happen.

Preface

The theories of Charles Darwin, Sigmund Freud, and Havelock Ellis had a profound impact on the modern world. Evidence of this is apparent not only in the sciences but also in architecture, in philosophy, and in the arts. While these sexological theories have dramatically altered the way we think and act, they have also given us new language with which to speak and nowhere is that language more apparent than in the texts of the moderns. The "tangled evolutionary garden" becomes a recurring image in modern texts and is articulated in works too numerous to name. Darwin's language has become a distinct part of the fabric of English; so, too, has the language of his successor Sigmund Freud. The names of Oedipus and Electra are more often associated with sexual fixations than they ever were with the ancient Greeks and one only has to say the words "Freudian slip" to denote an underlying motivation for making a mistake. And although Havelock Ellis is no longer as well known as he once was, many still recognize the term "sexual inversion" as homosexuality.

Strangely enough, while psychoanalytic readings have become commonplace in the field of critical inquiry relating to modern texts, few critics have actually made the connection that to accept psychoanalytic premises, one must recognize Darwin's theories, for they are the very basis on which Freud founded his theory. Ultimately, Darwin is the source for most sexological theories and yet he is perhaps the least discussed in relation to literature. With this study, I hope to make a case for Darwin's presence in the texts of Hemingway and H.D. as both writers examined what it meant to be man or woman in the modern era. Along with Darwin, I will also discuss the presence of Ellis and Freud, as they employed much of his theory in the creation of their own.

By incorporating contemporary theories into their presentation of character, Hemingway and H.D. demonstrate a keen awareness of the complex biological and psychological motivations for human social behavior. The texts they wrought in the modern era are testimony to the heavy influence of sexological theories. Evolutionary thought and psychological examination seemed to be in the air in the 20s and these two authors exemplify the pervasiveness of both. While the authors attempt to define and describe human behavior and the motivation for it, they also present characters whose sexuality is often not in keeping with the gender traits they display. Further, both Hemingway and H.D. create characters whose genders seem to change; at one moment, we see characters like Catherine Bourne in *The Garden of Eden* displaying distinctly "feminine" behavior. Doting on her husband David, Catherine often appears as the epitome of the feminine wife, desiring only to please and admire him. At other points in the novel, however, Catherine cuts her hair "like a man," wears David's clothes and has sex with a woman. Brett Ashley likewise displays an uncanny femininity; even as she can "drink like a man," Brett (whose name alone gives one "gender" pause) is most distinctly female with her curvaceous figure and demanding sexuality.

In *Paint it Today*, H.D. presents us with Josepha whose eyes "Angelo would have garnered in a group of holy boys, copied for one face and re-created for another" but whose eyes are also the "eyes of a Messalina" (9). Josepha often behaves boyishly and commandingly and yet is also "a girl;" this blending of gender traits is often described by H.D. as "unwholesome" even as her heroine Midget cannot be swayed in her adoration of Josepha. *Hermione* is also peopled with characters whose genders and sexuality are ambiguous and changing. Her Gart, the main character, describes herself as "nebulous" and the self-description is appropriate. The persistent blurring and shifting of gender is nearly constant in the texts of both Hemingway and H.D.; I argue here that this persistence is a direct result of the authors' close examination of sexological theories.

Emphasizing biological drives as the primary forces behind human behavior, Hemingway created characters who illustrate Darwin's explanation of the need to kill and eat in "the survival of the fittest," and who also demonstrate his theory of the process of sexual selection undertaken by females in the drive toward procreation. Although H.D. didn't credit human behavior as being biologically determined, she did believe strongly in psychology and psychoanalysis, which have evolutionary theory at their roots. H.D.'s novels are mainly chronicles of the psychological state of her main characters and often, these main characters are thinly veiled versions of her. Further, even as she argued against Darwin's theories, H.D. often employed his terminology and made many links in her poetry and prose between the plant, animal, and human worlds.

Both H.D. and Hemingway complicate their presentation of instinctual behaviors by including in their texts the presence of sexually and morally ambivalent characters. Clouding the drives to hunt, to kill and eat, and to select with the desire for morality and heroism, Hemingway and H.D.

create characters reflective of a fusion of Darwin's sexual and evolutionary theories with Ellis' more metaphysical theories of love, inversion and sexual compulsion. These characters also often exhibit traits evocative of Freud's psychoanalytic theories of sexual fixation, obsession, transference, and conflict. My study focuses on the ways in which Hemingway and H.D. explain human behavior through the sexual complexity of their characters and how this complexity exemplifies contemporary sexual theories, for sexuality and its "shifting" is at the heart of both authors' work.

Introduction:
"Strange Bedfellows"

> Unless we comprehend the exact process which is being worked out beneath the shifting and multifold phenomena presented to us we can never hope to grasp in their true relations any of the normal or abnormal manifestations of this instinct.
> —Havelock Ellis

The connections between H.D. and Ernest Hemingway are not, at first glance, obvious and when I began this study, I contemplated whether or not a case could be made linking such strange literary bedfellows. However, while they appear an "odd coupling," these two writers have much in common biographically, philosophically, and psychologically. Their similarities become apparent when selected works of Hemingway and H.D. are examined through the lens of contemporary theories of evolution and human sexuality. The theories of Charles Darwin, Sigmund Freud, and Havelock Ellis were the rubrics used by Hemingway and H.D. as both writers examined what it meant to be man or woman in the modern era. By incorporating contemporary theories into their presentation of character, Hemingway and H.D. demonstrate a desire to "examine the exact process which is being worked out beneath the shifting and multifold phenomena" comprising human sexuality that Ellis refers to in the epigraph above. Their acute awareness of the complex biological and psychological motivations for human behavior is at the heart of both writers' work as is the confusion resulting from gender expectations and deviations from them.

With an emphasis on biological drives as the primary forces behind human behavior, Hemingway created characters who illustrate Darwin's argument that the lives of all biological species are driven by "a struggle for existence" (*The Origin of Species* 53) which depends on a cycle of killing, eating, and procreating. His evolutionary theory shattered the image of man as king of the natural world, and the social and historic impact of *The Origin of Species* and *The Descent of Man* was very great. Darwin's "reduction" of humans to the level of other natural organisms, rather than privileging them to a higher status, felled with one blow countless years of religious and philosophical posturing. Further, his insistence on the importance of the female in the process of sexual selection deconstructed the myth of the sexually passive female.

While Darwin's evolutionary theories are the basis for H.D.'s and Hemingway's explanation for human behavior, both authors complicate their presentation of these instinctual behaviors by including in their texts the presence of sexually and morally ambivalent characters. The drives to hunt, to kill and eat, and to select are often presented alongside desires for morality, heroism, selflessness, and true romantic love; these seemingly conflicting ideals result in characters reflective of a fusion of Darwin's sexual and evolutionary theories with Ellis's more metaphysical theories of love, inversion, and sexual compulsion.

Ellis agreed with Darwin's evolutionary theory that

> [h]e who is not content to look, like a savage, at the phenomena of nature as disconnected, cannot any longer believe that man is the work of a separate act of creation. He will be forced to admit that the close resemblance of the embryo of man to that, for instance, of a dog—the construction of the skull, limbs and whole frame on the same plan with that of other mammals, independently of the uses to which the parts may be put—the occasional re-appearance of various structures, for instance of several muscles, which man does not normally possess, but which are common to the Quadrumana—and a crowd of analogous facts—all point in the plainest manner to the conclusion that man is the co-descendant with other mammals of a common progenitor. (*Descent of Man* 909-10)

and further that

> [s]exual selection [. . .] has played an important part in the history of the organic world [. . .] In the lower divisions of the animal kingdom, sexual selection seems to have done nothing: such animals are often affixed for life to the same spot, or have the sexes combined in the same individual, or what is still more important, their perceptive and intellectual faculties are not sufficiently advance to allow of the feelings of love and jealousy, or of the exertion of choice. When, however, we come to the Arthropoda and Vertebrata, even to the lowest classes in these two great Sub-kingdoms, sexual selection has effected much. (*Descent of Man* 910)

However, while Ellis agreed to the theory of a "common progenitor" and to the notion that primarily, women were most frequently the selectors in the act of sex and that this selection was crucial to man's development and success, Ellis also believed that in the case of humans, sexual love could contain an intangible or spiritual element. The sexologist believed that in fact, the sexual act between two lovers resulted in a sort of spiritual elevation. For example, even as Ellis describes the aroused sexual instinct

Introduction

(tumescence) as a biological response to stimuli, as does Darwin, Ellis further explains that

> [a]t the same time, it is probable, we are exploring the mystery which underlies all the subtle appreciations, all the emotional undertones, which are woven in the web of the whole world as it appeals to us through those sensory passages by which alone it can reach us. We are here approaching, therefore, a fundamental subject of unsurpassable importance, a subject which has not yet been accurately explored save at a few isolated points . . . (*Studies in the Psychology of Sex* 1:3 2)

Ellis's description of sex as an almost mystical and monumentally important subject is in complete agreement with the presentation of sex in the works of H.D. and Hemingway. Time after time, the texts of both authors revolve around sexual relationships and the problems that often ensue because of their failure. This failure is often due to the inability of one character to successfully have sex, the sexual object choice is the same sex, the infidelity of one or more characters, or the fact that the sexual relationship is so consuming that it results in neurotic or obsessive behavior. For Hemingway and H.D. it would seem that "sex is the central problem of life" (Ellis *Preface, Studies in the Psychology of Sex*).

While the works of H.D. and Hemingway evince an awareness and agreement of Ellis's ideas regarding sex, the characters both authors create are complicated by their Freudian behavior, as well. Characters, particularly sexually ambivalent ones, often exhibit traits evocative of Freud's psychoanalytical theories of sexual fixation with particular regard to the mother complex. Freud articulates this fixation in his notes, stating that

> the later inverts go through in their childhood a phase of very intense but short-lived fixation on the woman (usually the mother) and after overcoming it, they identify themselves with the woman and take themselves as the sexual object; that is, proceeding on a narcissistic basis, they look for young men resembling themselves in persons whom they wish to love as their mother has loved them. (*Basic Writings of Sigmund Freud* 560n)

While "boyish" men are not common in the works of H.D., boyish women *are*; both Midget and Josepha exhibit a boyishness, as do Her Gart and Fayne Rabb. However, Hemingway does present effeminate men, such as those occupying the Cafe Select in *The Sun Also Rises* and often makes references to unmanly men and his distaste for them. These characters have not gone unnoticed by critics and there has been much speculation regarding Hemingway's possibly latent homosexual desires resulting perhaps from his ties to his mother; H.D. likewise has been discussed as having a strong desire for her mother's affection. In fact, both H.D. and Hemingway were so greatly influenced by their mothers that numerous critics have pointed out both authors' tendency to seek sexual partners who projected character traits strongly associated with their mothers. It is not surprising, then, that H.D. and Hemingway project many of these traits onto their fictional characters. The inability of Hemingway (and H.D.) to completely "let go" of the mother's image as associated with sexual object selection seems to further illustrate Freud's mother complex which states that

> [t]he man seeks above all the memory picture of his mother as it has dominated him since the beginning of childhood; this is quite consistent with the fact that the mother, if still living, strives against this, her renewal, and meets it with hostility. In view of this significance of the infantile relation to the parents for the later selection of the sexual object, it is easy to understand that every disturbance of this infantile relation brings to a head the most serious results for the sexual life after puberty. (*The Basic Writings of Sigmund Freud* 618-19)

Although it is impossible to say which theorist held greater sway with H.D. or Hemingway at any given time, it is important to realize that the work of Ellis and Freud could not have occurred without Darwin's establishment of the evolutionary premise, as explained at length by Lucille Ritvo. Ritvo argues that Freud's theories of psychoanalysis are built directly on Charles Darwin's sexual and evolutionary theories and asserts that Darwin not only directly influenced Freud but that the two scientists' works would have the same societal impact, as well as suffer the same misreading. Ritvo states that

> [t]he life of the creator of psychoanalysis coincides almost exactly with the onset of the "Darwinian revolution." Freud's life and work reveal the impact and also the vicissitudes of the new theory. Fossilized in the extensive corpus of Freud's writings is the evolutionary theory of Darwin's day, including aspects expunged by time. Freud's own theory became subject to surprisingly similar misinterpretations and assaults. (1)

She further explains that while Freud and Darwin never met, they shared close associations in the scientific community, particularly during Freud's early days as a zoologist. The young Freud read the first unedited and credible German translations of Darwin's work, and as Ritvo states, "Freud's references to Darwin are of" an "idealized and unambivalent nature" (17). Although Freud does not directly credit Darwin in relation to his psychological works, he does acknowledge the great naturalist's important contributions to science in general. Freud stated that "the theories of Darwin, which were then of topical interest, strongly attracted me, for they held out hopes of an extraordinary advance in our understanding of the world" (*An Autobiographical Study*). Freud's firm belief in the work of Charles Darwin makes acceptance of his psychoanalytic theories dependent upon an assumption of evolutionary ideals.

Like Freud, Ellis also grounds his work in Darwin's theories, footnoting him profusely in many of his works, as well as freely adopting the use of many Darwinian terms. One crucial difference between Darwin's and Ellis's approach to the explanation of sexual behavior, however, is Ellis's belief in the transcendental properties of human sexual contact. As noted, unlike Darwin, even while Ellis believed that sexual relationships were often the root of many of life's problems, he also felt that while human sexual contact was a direct result of instinctual desires, the sex act itself when undertaken elevated the male and female involved to an almost spiritual realm. Ellis's claim to the transcendental quality of sex would appeal to the ethereal H.D., but the pragmatic Hemingway would find it harder to accept. Instead, Hemingway would be drawn more closely to Ellis's case studies, such as those in *The Dance of Life*, and more particularly, those involving sexual obsessions such as *Erotic Symbolism*.

While H.D. and Hemingway explore the importance of sexual theories as explanations for human behavior, they also examine gender as a culturally constructed, fluctuating dynamic. Both authors illustrate the instability of sexual and personal identity when gender traits are reassigned, as in *The Garden of Eden* and *Kora and Ka*, for example. The instability of identity, the capacity for transformation, the self as fluid and often progressive, all are related concepts which appear frequently in the works of Hemingway and H.D. as they explore both the genesis and metamorphosis of identity. I attribute the persistent presentation of sexual identity as fluid to H.D.'s and Hemingway's knowledge of "man's ancient bisexual nature," an idea crucial to the sexual theories of Darwin, Ellis, and Freud (Sulloway 158-9). The continual, yet futile, quest for a stable identity pursued by Hemingway and H.D. is most evident in *Paint it Today, Hermione, Bid Me to Live,* and *The Sea Garden*, by H.D., and *The Garden of Eden, The Sun Also Rises, For Whom the Bell Tolls,* and "The Sea Change" by Hemingway.

My purpose in illustrating a shared awareness of sex theories and the instability of identity in the works of these two authors, one male, one female, is twofold: first, to deconstruct the myths alleging Ernest Hemingway's misogyny and morbid preoccupation with masculinity, and second, to illustrate the distinct similarities in the theoretical premise of works written by men and women in the modern era. By reading Hemingway with and through H.D. (the influence of contemporary sexual and evolutionary theories ever in mind), Hemingway's texts illustrate an acute awareness of the struggle for meaning, for purpose, for identity, a struggle shared equally by both sexes. They no longer appear morbidly preoccupied with "male" identity; instead, his works are evocative of a deep knowledge of the "bisexual" natures of men and women. Similarly, by reading H.D. with and through Hemingway, her openly homoerotic prose texts are evidence of the close relationship of sexuality, self-identity, and artistic creativity; the fusion of sexuality and self-perception with creativity evidenced in her texts is acutely reminiscent of Hemingway. This similarity is important both as evidence that male and female modern authors were struggling with the concept of defining a sexual and artistic self, and as a catalyst for closer scrutiny of H.D.'s prose works. Her insistent questioning of human behavior and subsequent search for explanation in the realms of contemporary sex theories are so consistent with Hemingway, the near-exclusion of her prose works from the modern American literary canon seems unusual.

Chapter One constitutes a brief discussion of the historical situation in America immediately preceding the publication of Hemingway's and H.D.'s early work and addresses the increasingly popular interest in contemporary sexual theories. The work done by Elaine Showalter ("Syphilis, Sexuality, and the Fiction of the Fin de Siecle"), Eve Sedgwick (*Epistemology of the Closet, Tendencies*), and Teresa De Lauretis (*The Practice of Love*) on early-twentieth century sexuality is the foundation for much of my argument here; not less important, however, are texts by D'Emilio and Freeman (*Intimate Matters*), Gilbert and Gubar (*The Madwoman in the Attic*), and Jay and Glasgow (*Lesbian Texts and Contexts*), for their emphasis on the social evolution of sexuality. The changing nature of sexuality and the subsequent social reaction which ensued informs my later discussion of the numerous biographical similarities between H.D. and Hemingway and posits an explanation for the profound influence of contemporary sexual and biological theories in their work. While I draw on theorists such as those named above whose work is grounded in the social evolution of human sexuality, it is not my purpose to examine Hemingway and H.D. through the psychological and sexological lenses of late-twentieth century theorists. Rather, my purpose is to examine them through the lenses that are most crucial to Hemingway's and H.D.'s own era.

Consequently, much of the evidence for my hypothesis that Hemingway and H.D. were acutely affected by contemporary biological theories of sexuality is derived from the detailed works on these authors' early lives by biographers Kenneth Lynn, Barbara Guest, and Mark Spilka, who all agree on the important influence both authors' androgynous early upbringing had on their later work, as well as to the importance of what these authors read. Growing up in households heavily influenced by science, both Hemingway and H.D. read numerous scientific texts, including the works of Darwin, Ellis, and later, Freud.

Freud's "discovery" of the id, the ego, and the superego; his articulation of Oedipal and Electral fixations; his hypotheses regarding psychological stages of development and arrest; and his terminology for discussing sexuality in general, gave the late-nineteenth and early-twentieth centuries the language to discuss the changing nature of human sexuality. Likewise,

Ellis's case studies chronicling human sexuality forced issues such as bisexuality, androgyny, inversion, and sexual fetishism to the forefront of psychological studies. Most importantly, however, the work done in the study of human sexuality by Freud and Ellis could not have been accomplished without the groundbreaking sexual and evolutionary theories articulated by Charles Darwin. These three "sexologists" theoretically framed the ongoing discussion of sex that preoccupied late-nineteenth and early-twentieth century society; their texts greatly influenced the lives and works of H.D. and Hemingway as they struggled to understand and explain human behavior.

Chapter Two extends the discussion of biographical similarities between Hemingway and H.D. in the context of the expatriation of both authors and expatriation's relevance to their work. As Americans abroad, H.D. and Hemingway became members of a clique of writers and artists exploring new forms. In Europe H.D. would meet other women writers, many of whom were practicing bisexuals or lesbians, and the impact of their open sexual expression on the Moravian farm girl was profound. Part of the same social circle, Hemingway also made the acquaintance of numerous authors, among them, F. Scott Fitzgerald and Ezra Pound. These literary connections were crucial to the development of H.D. and Hemingway as writers; it was with these other expatriated writers that H.D. and Hemingway would share their work and their ideas, including their interest in science and its relation to sexual and emotional behavior.

Perhaps the most influential writer in Paris for H.D. and Hemingway, indeed, for all the moderns, was Gertrude Stein. Stein is one of the most direct ties binding H.D. and Hemingway, for they were both occasional attendees at her weekly salon. At the evening gatherings, Stein would act as literary, intellectual, and artistic critic; her knowledge of scientific theories, her determined explorations with language, her appreciation for artistic change, her insistence on leading her own sexual and national life, and her celebration of love in an era seemingly devoid of it were qualities which made her hugely important in the lives of the moderns. Association with Stein and her ideas helped both H.D. and Hemingway articulate their own artistic and ideological explorations.

Like Stein, Hemingway and H.D. experienced a changing sense of national identity while in Europe; H.D.'s national sympathies changed so abruptly that several critics argue that she married English poet Richard Aldington in part to become a British citizen. Hemingway, to a lesser degree, questioned his national sympathies, contemplating America's political ideologies and foreign policies during his early days in Paris. Simultaneous with this political questioning was a deeper artistic one; Hemingway would often examine closely his ability to write about home only when away from it. Their experiences as Americans in Europe intensified H.D.'s and Hemingway's awareness of shifting identity; the influence of other expatriated writers work, as well as the exposure to these writers' often sexually ambiguous or dysfunctional lives, helped contextualize H.D.'s and Hemingway's explorations of self, sexuality, and meaning.

Evidence for the profound impact of expatriation is most acute in the "war" stories of H.D. and Hemingway; where one is during a war, who one sides with, how this can change and how one changes because of it, are persistent questions for both authors. These questions are often linked to sexual identity, particularly in *Bid Me To Live, A Farewell to Arms*, and numerous Hemingway short stories. I focus on several texts by Hemingway and H.D. in the second part of chapter two as I discuss the increasing momentum of identity "slippage" and transformation the further these authors move away both physically and mentally from their original geographic "homes."

Crucial to my discussion of expatriation and national "dualism" are works by Andrea Weiss (*Paris Was a Woman*) and Shari Benstock (*Women of the Left Bank*) which chronicle the American artist's experience in modern Europe. Also integral to my discussion in this chapter is Stephen Cooper's description of the development of Hemingway's political and social conscience (*The Politics of Ernest Hemingway*).

In Chapter Three I present a reading of Hemingway's *The Garden of Eden* through the lenses of Darwin, Ellis, and Freud, arguing that Hemingway's sexually ambivalent characters in the novel reflect his absorption in and subsequent translation of contemporary sexual theories. I question the myths regarding his homophobia and misogyny. While I do not attempt to argue against Hemingway's negative portrayal of homosexuals, I do wish to complicate the reading of this portrayal, for Hemingway's "homophobia" has been both overemphasized and oversimplified. Through a reading of characters such as Catherine and David Bourne from *The Garden of Eden*, I attempt in this chapter to illustrate Hemingway's struggle to bear witness to the modern awareness of androgyny, sexual ambivalence, and homosexuality. Here and elsewhere I argue that Hemingway's negative view of homosexuality was a response to Darwin, one that verifies Eve Sedgwick's ideas of "homosexual panic." In my lengthy analysis of *The Garden of Eden*, I suggest that, while it is the culmination of his lifelong contemplation of human sexual behavior, the manuscript's unfinished state reflects his underlying sense that theories of sexuality and identity are, like sex itself, given to further evolutionary change.

Much contemporary criticism of androgynous or sexually ambivalent characters in Hemingway's work links the existence of these characters to his early childhood, during which the young Hemingway was dressed and raised as a "twin" to elder sister, Marcelline. While the impact of his androgynous upbringing, critically examined by Mark Spilka (*Hemingway's Quarrel With Androgyny*), and Comley and Scholes

(*Hemingway's Genders*), is compelling and I will discuss it briefly here, Hemingway's presentation of androgyny and other aspects of human sexuality is also profoundly impacted by his early reading of sex theories. Because Hemingway's presentation of sexual ambivalence is based on Darwin's theory of bisexuality, as well as Ellis' theories of inversion and erotic symbolism, I deal with these theories in depth. Chapter Three will also discuss Hemingway's more veiled Freudian imagery. Possible explanations for Hemingway's persistent denial of Freud's influence are offered here as well. Because much of Freud's work revolves around the phallus, the fear associated with its loss, and the latent homosexuality associated with male bonding, Hemingway perhaps feared that an association with Freud's work would implicate him as a potential sufferer of latent desires. Ironically, by negating Freud's psychoanalytic theory yet subsequently implementing many of its elements in his work, Hemingway inadvertently engaged in very "Freudian" behavior: he engaged in the reflex mechanism of denial integral to his homosocial acceptance.

In Chapter Four I address H.D.'s texts which are similarly occupied by sexually ambivalent characters and who likewise behave in a manner articulated in the works of Darwin, Ellis, and Freud; unlike Hemingway, however, H.D.'s characters repeatedly attempt to explain themselves in the psychoanalytic terms of Freud. The impact of Freud is much more obvious in the work of H.D. as is that of Ellis, possibly because H.D. had a personal relationship with Ellis for an extended period and maintained a patient-analyst relationship with Freud for nearly two years. While H.D. maintained a relationship with Ellis (they traveled together several times and maintained a correspondence for many years), it was never as deep nor emotionally important as the one she had with Freud. Although Ellis had many important ideas, to H.D., Freud was the true genius.

H.D.'s blatant incorporation of sexual theories and autobiography into her prose works is a calculated departure from the strict confines of much of her poetry. It appears to be an attempt at effecting what Dianne Chisholm calls Freud's "writing cure" (15). This idea seems applicable to all of H.D.'s prose works that are intensely autobiographical and seem to have been produced more for the well being of the author than the audience. Although H.D. did not undergo psychoanalysis with Freud until 1933-34, she was reading Freud and "revising" his theories years earlier. Freud's insistence on the necessity of autobiographical writing and completing a "straight narrative without embellishment" (Chisholm 69) resulted in a prose oeuvre which chronicles H.D.'s life and the lives of the moderns she knew. While this "life writing" may have aided H.D. in her search for self, it is also an invaluable tool for contemporary scholars seeking a deeper understanding of the modern era.

H.D. and Hemingway draw on biological and psychological theories not only to portray certain characters' sexual ambivalence, but more importantly, certain characters' struggles with sexual dysfunction. The childless bisexual or androgynous characters might, for example, suggest the authors' awareness of Darwin's theory of sterility among hybrids. The sexually dysfunctional characters (such as Jake Barnes in *The Sun Also Rises* and Julia in *Bid Me To Live*), however, seem much more tied to Freud's theories relating to war neuroses. With eerie similarity, the main characters produced by H.D. and Hemingway in these two novels are arguably manifestations of the authors themselves, tortured as they were by war. Both were "wounded" during WWI, H.D. losing father and brother to death around that time, miscarrying a child (and subsequently nearly losing her own life during a second pregnancy), as well as losing her husband to another woman; Hemingway receiving serious physical wounds to his legs and subsequently losing the love of his life, nurse Agnes Kurowsky, to an affair with a European count.

The serious physical and psychic trauma caused by the war would haunt both authors for the rest of their lives. Kenneth Lynn affirms Hemingway's knowledge of this, citing him as confessing that "the wound" he'd suffered "had so deeply affected him that he had spent his whole life as a writer composing variations on the story of the psychically crippled 'sick man'" (*Hemingway* 106). H.D. likewise was aware that she had never fully recovered from the wounds of war; Susan Friedman explains that "[w]ar, death, masculine insensitivity and betrayal became completely interwoven in H.D.'s mind" and further, that the events of WWI would replay themselves in H.D.'s subconscious years later. "When Hugh Dowding 'repudiated' their spiritual companionship just after the bombing ceased, the war terrors repressed for nearly thirty years returned to cause another severe breakdown" (*Psyche Reborn* 29-30).

While it is fascinating to note the distinctly similar responses to war in the case of these two moderns, it is also vitally important to note that the characters created to represent the authors' experience over and over again were writers who often appeared sexually dysfunctional. Seemingly, while H.D. and Hemingway both outwardly acknowledged that war had a profound impact on them as individuals, it had also both inspired and crippled their writing. The Julia of *Bid Me to Live*, for example, is so sexually paralyzed by the war that she does not prevent her husband from taking another woman upstairs. While in several scenes in the novel Julia and Rafe appear to have sex, it seems more a desperate attempt to keep him on her part than it does a pleasurable experience. Indeed, Julia finds it hard to understand how anyone can seek pleasure of any kind during wartime. Jake Barnes in *The Sun Also Rises* is an even more overt example of the war's impact on Hemingway as a writer for Barnes *is* a writer, a writer who has received a wound preventing him from having sex again. Throughout the course of the novel, Jake flirts with Brett Ashley with the same impotence that he flirts with writing; nothing, apparently, ever comes of it. The continual tying of war to writing and to sex lies at the root of both authors' creative energy. Seemingly, they appear to understand that while sexuality is crucially tied to identity, it is equally entangled in the act of writing. The persistent linking of writing, sexuality, and ultimately, self-perception, is the most important shared element in the works of these two authors. Chapter Five therefore focuses on how persistent is the linking of language with self in the works of both authors, how evocative of contemporary sexual theories that language is, and further, how these two authors use sexual dysfunction as a metaphor for their difficulties with language and writing.

By demonstrating the influential presence of contemporary biological and psychological theories in Hemingway and H.D.'s work, I wish to illustrate that these moderns' need to decipher the self in relation to science was an obsession. Without an understanding of the importance of contemporary theories of evolution and human sexuality, any reading of the texts by Hemingway and H.D. is incomplete.

In making my case that H.D. and Hemingway drew on contemporary science in their fictional explanations of human sexual identity, I will draw briefly from ideas presented by psychologist Kenneth Gergen whose text *The Saturated Self* chronicles the dynamic relationships that exist between art, science, and culture. Gergen points out that these "relationships pull us in myriad directions, inviting us to play such a variety of roles that the very concept of an 'authentic' self with knowable characteristics recedes from view. The fully saturated self becomes no self at all" (6-7). Gergen's comments are particularly insightful with regard to Hemingway and H.D. as neither author could establish an identity that would hold. Text after text written by these two moderns illustrate their continual transformation and evolution; their works chronicle a progression from hopeful idealism and desire for married happiness to restless depression and distrust in relationships. Their fictional works also mirror the authors' creative metamorphoses as writers. Both initially began as writers of short works, but as their lives changed, becoming more complex personally, ideologically and artistically, their art forms were forced to change also. Caught up as they were in the excitement and confusion which comprised the cultural move to take in Darwin, Freud, and Ellis, coupled with their experiences with war, H.D. and Hemingway increasingly incorporated sexology and psychology into their work.

Because of the relative absence of studies such as mine, the intertextual connections illustrated in this examination reveal new insights into Hemingway, H.D., and the collection of works we discuss as modern American literature. Moreover, while my primary purpose is to examine the persistent presence of contemporary evolutionary and sexual theories in the works of H.D. and Hemingway, a secondary purpose is to focus critical attention on H.D.'s modernist fiction. When discussed at all, H.D.'s fictional work is often presented as a mass of unreadable, meandering, and self-indulgent autobiography (it is interesting to note that this description of H.D.'s prose closely resembles many critical descriptions of Hemingway's later work). Instead of being critiqued as a novelist, she is primarily discussed as a poet, and her established place in the canon is that of the queen of poetic Imagism, a short-lived but nonetheless well cited period in modern poetics.

Although H.D.'s early poetry was earmarked as the best of the Imagist era by Ezra Pound and Marianne Moore, reducing H.D.'s role in the modernist canon to that of an Imagist poet is both disturbing and problematic. H.D.'s poetic career was lifelong and her works encompassed many styles other than Imagism. As Gary Burnett points out, her "auspicious beginning" as Imagist poet

> was to do as much harm as good to H.D.'s reputation. It did present her to the public in a context almost tailor-made for her earliest, 'laconic' poems, but it also locked her critical reaction into the narrow boundaries defined by the Imagist manifesto. (1)

H.D. wrote fiction from 1911 until her death in 1961. While the earliest works "Lady Leicester" and "The Griffin of Temple Bar" were short stories, in 1921 H.D. wrote *Paint it Today*, her first novel. Like much of her later poetry, H.D.'s prose works are often overlooked and given little canonical recognition. The exclusion of H.D. from all discussion of the modern novel has been a massive oversight which seems strange, for as Claire Buck points out in her discussion of the prose fiction H.D. produced in the 1920s and 30s, "novel after novel reiterates the female version of the traditional modernist narrative of the portrait of the artist as a young man" (13).

Rather than an oversight, however, the omission of H.D.'s fiction instead appears to be the result of an exclusion based on a relatively consistent canonical preference for texts presented in a clear and linear narrative form, and whose gaze is predominantly male. Although H.D.'s novels address similar themes and characters as those written by other moderns, Hemingway in particular, they are so overtly female, so engrossed with the notion of woman-as-artist, as author, that her novels are not included in the canon. While it has been argued that H.D.'s style was simply too unwieldy and formless for modern tastes, a case can be made for American writers who broke from a linear and chronological modern form, most notably William Faulkner whose prose "experiments," including multiple narrators ("As I Lay Dying") and time as linked to perception rather than chronology (*The Sound and the Fury*), are a radical departure from most modern American texts. However, while the form of Faulkner's work was highly experimental and non-traditional, the narrators' viewpoints are not. Ultimately, each narrator in Faulkner's works views life from a "traditional," primarily heterosexual, and distinctly "male" gaze. While H.D.'s non-traditional form might have been acceptable to modern tastes, the unrelenting female gaze of H.D.'s prose seems too radical for canonical inclusion.

Susan Friedman explains H.D.'s canonical omission as a problem shared by other female moderns. As signifiers of desire and central objects of the masculine modern text, women were subjects in rather than producers of modern texts. She writes: "[w]oman, or the desire for her, fueled the process of modernist representations and marked its avant-garde forms. By itself, however, this gendered modernism leaves out the story of women-as-writers in its production" (2). Friedman asserts that so long as H.D. or any other woman insisted on writing texts where woman is central, where the world is witnessed from and through her view, that her texts (and the texts of other female moderns) would be invalidated. Friedman's ideas seem to echo Gilbert and Gubar's explanation for female exclusion from the canon as unsurprising, for "the patriarchal notion that the writer 'fathers' his text just as God fathered the world is and has been all-pervasive in Western literary civilization" (4). While Gilbert and Gubar primarily address the Victorian era, the modern one closely following appears relatively unchanged. Modern texts are, for the most part, male gendered texts; as Friedman points out, this leaves women's consciousness and experience underrepresented in the recognized American modern canon. To rectify the situation, a female gendered "reading" of modernism is necessary.

Claire Buck also insists on a female-gendered reading of modernism, claiming that to exclude female and minority writers from the modern canon is to construct a "selective tradition" comprised of a "particular and gendered set of practices which have been normalized as the only modernism" (3). The canonical recognition of H.D.'s poetry where the narrator's gender is less overt, less obviously female, as is often the object of the narrator's gaze, and the subsequent dismissal of her female-oriented works, supports Buck's argument of a "selective tradition."

H.D.'s gendered feminist narrative should be reconsidered for canonical placement first on its own merit and second as part of the growing awareness of gender's dynamic nature and its importance as a cultural construct and descriptor of identity. With the inclusion of novels such as those written by H.D., whose narrative style is best described as "stream of consciousness" and whose gaze is clearly female, the notion of a homogenous American "modern" style will be put to rest. Rather than dismiss H.D.'s fictional work, we should include it in an effort to make the canon of modern American fiction more reflective of the literary richness of the early modern period. The inclusion of H.D.'s prose may also act as a catalyst for dismembering the misperception of her poetic works as texts of icy, genderless purity by providing the audience for her poetry with the information to decode her poems. Too frequently, H.D.'s gendered encoded meanings are misinterpreted as symbols which fit the restricting confines of the Imagist poem, with its often unspecified, unnamed speaker and timeless, mythological construct. Claire Buck explains H.D.'s seeming omission of gender in this way: gender "disappears from the poem as a content, excised by the modernist and Imagist precept of impersonality, but reappears in an encoded form" (14). Only by decoding the symbols in which H.D. has hidden her meaning can the reader ascertain the underlying theme of many of H.D.'s early poems. Reading H.D.'s poetry through the persona she reveals in her prose gives the reader the satisfaction of "knowing" a part of H.D. and destroys any lingering doubts about the frigidity of her poetic works. Moreover, because so many of her prose works describe her contemporaries and the work they produced, these biographical insights contribute to our knowledge of the modern era. As Janice Robinson remarks,

> H.D. was not only an extraordinarily autobiographical writer, but also an acutely accurate recorder of detail. Since the cast of characters of the Imagist group was such prolific writers, we can learn much about the history of the period if we read their literature in relation to one another. (xiv)

Many will argue that the canonical inclusion of H.D.'s Imagist poetry is sufficient representation of her work. However, because H.D.'s Imagist poetry is not obviously evocative of her femininity, the modern female experience remains marginalized. As Lillian Robinson points out, "the apparently systematic neglect of women's experience in the literary canon . . . takes the form of distorting and misreading a few recognized female writers and excluding the others" (106). I would argue that H.D. is just such a case of critical distortion and misreading.

Reading H.D.'s novels with those written by Hemingway puts her work in critical perspective. Her novels are quests for identity and meaning, as are his. Examining H.D.'s novels alongside those of Hemingway is an effort to revise the modern canon so that it may reflect the increasingly popular theory that American modernism wore many stylistic faces. As Friedman remarks in her discussion of the need for female canonical representation,

> Gendering modernism-reading gender in modernism-needs to weave together these different strands of how it was (en)gendered. The tendency in male modernism to fix women in the silent space of the feminine meant that many female modernists had to release themselves from this linguistic trap as the (pre)condition of their speech. (Friedman 3)

By reading several of H.D.'s fictional works in tandem with selected works by Ernest Hemingway, all of which I believe share similar themes of sexual and philosophical questioning, the "weaving together" Friedman refers to can begin. Through a close reading of these authors' texts, the "universal" themes of love, death, and survival become apparent, as do the authors' gendered perspectives. When examined together, the characters these writers created and the texts they inhabit gain a great deal. By untangling the complex web of H.D.'s novels, we often glimpse female characters in her works such as Julia Ashton, who bear a striking resemblance to Hemingway's unheroic protagonists like Jake Barnes. These characters tread the path of the modern world in the same tortured and questioning manner. They are on quests for meaning and purpose in a world that seems devoid of either, and while the writing is stylistically very different, the philosophical premise of the works these characters inhabit is strikingly similar. Both H.D. and Hemingway sought to make sense of their world by reading and interpreting contemporary scientific theories of life, love, and sex, and while H.D.'s work is unquestionably more metaphysical in its overtones, the controlling elements which propel the plots of both writers are undoubtedly Darwinian.

While the linking of H.D. with Hemingway validates her prose works, the similarities in the presentation of female and sexually ambivalent characters in the works of both authors sheds much light on Hemingway's texts as well. Rather than perceive Hemingway as a misogynist in his creation of female characters who either die, take secondary positions to men, or operate as "she-devils," after reading the characters through the lens of sexual theories, Hemingway's females seem something else entirely. Instead of the one-dimensional women so often proposed, these characters are rather interpretations and incarnations of the theories Hemingway read. They are motivated, just as his male characters are, by instinctual and subsequently psychological drives. When read in this way, Hemingway's female characters reveal an author who has "been misread and misinterpreted by enthusiasts and detractors alike" (Lynn 10). Particularly when reading the posthumous *The Garden of Eden* through the lens of contemporary sexual theories, Hemingway's sexual and philosophical complexity as well as his acute human sensitivity is revealed. I hope to prove biographer Kenneth Lynn correct in his assumption that "[f]rom the very first, his best work was infused by more sensitive and complicated feelings about himself and the world than the stereotypes of Hemingway criticism have ever allowed" (Lynn 10).

H.D., too, has been frequently misread and misinterpreted. Perhaps, as Susan Friedman notes, H.D. was ahead of her time, for "fifty years before Helene Cixous and Luce Irigaray called for an ecriture feminine, for women to 'parler femme,' H.D. forged a prose discourse that wrote the female body and expanded the boundaries of the philosophical essay to inscribe it" (11). Unlike Cixous, however, H.D.'s attempts at advocating feminine literature and "body/spirit/mind" narrative were met with perplexity and criticism. Worthy of note is the particularly harsh treatment H.D. received at the hands of mentor Havelock Ellis upon his reading of H.D.'s *Notes on Thought and Vision*. Friedman claims that it was Ellis's negative criticism that was primarily responsible for H.D.'s decision not to seek a publisher for the essay. "Perhaps because of his response and the authority with which she had invested him, H.D. left the manuscript unpublished and never again tried to write an essay like *Notes on Thought and Vision*" (Friedman 12). However negative his criticism, H.D. would nevertheless maintain many of Ellis's psychological and sexual theories, incorporating them into a body of work that spanned her lifetime.

H.D.'s career as a writer lasted nearly fifty years, incorporating half a century of social commentary, artistic criticism, autobiography, and philosophical pondering. Her life and work discounts a popular concept that to be a woman and to be a modern writer were distinctly disparate identities. While many female moderns, Radclyffe Hall and Gertrude Stein, for example, considered domesticity and motherhood impossible obstacles to successful authorship, the reality is that all of these women made attempts at domestic partnerships which frequently lasted many years. Although many of the female moderns were primarily lesbian, several—Djuna Barnes, Collette, and Mina Loy, for instance— also had relationships with men, albeit unsuccessful ones. In the case of H.D., while her partnerships with men were fraught with indecision, infidelity, and inequality, her attachment to millionaire Winifred Ellerman (Bryher) lasted over forty years. Being both woman and writer was difficult; however, a brief glimpse at the lives of male writers at the time (whose attempts at domesticity also frequently met with disaster), makes this difficulty unsurprising. Finding the time to read, to contemplate and ultimately, to write, while maintaining a domestic relationship was not easy, regardless of the writer's gender. One has only to glance at the circumstances of Hemingway's life to see that he never succeeded in balancing the demands of authorship, fatherhood, and marriage.

Unlike female writers, however, authors such as Hemingway did not have to suffer the hindrance to their work caused by the artistic favoritism for the works of male authors who were perpetually held up as models of good literature. Few women are discussed as "first rank" modern novelists; during the modern era, many editors could not understand a great deal of American literature written by women, particularly works of "experimental" prose like that produced by H.D. and Gertrude Stein.

H.D. was among numerous women who did not seek or receive publication for many years; although writing constantly, even the female figure most closely associated with modernism, Gertrude Stein, was not printed by a major publishing house until 1924. Remarkably, while it was to Gertrude Stein Hemingway would turn for assistance, receiving the famous advice to "begin again and concentrate," it would be Hemingway who first attained true celebrity. It would seem that while Stein, like other female moderns, was appreciated personally and artistically, her work was misunderstood and frequently ignored by major publishers who could not conceptualize an audience for her work. Stein's predicament was common. The inability to conceptualize an audience for feminist narrative style was perhaps the most important reason for women's near-exclusion from the modern canon.

By restricting ourselves to a handful of modern texts by a small number of male writers, academe has falsely constructed one of the most productive periods of literary history. The assumption that the masculine styles accepted as representative of that time period were the only styles of value has invalidated numerous texts by women and minority writers, an important factor in the limitation of the modern American canon. By linking these two initially very different writers, by uniting them in a theme of discovery, of search for meaning, of interpreting their times, it is to be hoped that the vast chasm that formerly divided male and female modern American writers will, to some extent, be narrowed.

Sex Theories and the Shaping of Two Moderns

Chapter One

The Emergence of Two Moderns

> What hope or satisfaction could have been found in the Victorian concepts of order and religion had been devastated by industrialization and its resulting economic and social changes.
> —Linda Wagner-Martin

The twentieth century dawned on an America that was both economically and technologically successful. Making its mark on a country with vast potential in the form of labor and resources, the industrial revolution fulfilled the promise of experimental technology of the past fifty years. Once a wild and sparsely populated country, by 1900 the frontier had closed and America quickly became urbanized. Ruland and Bradbury note the importance of immense change in the organization of America and its populace in their work on the history of American literature, *From Puritanism to Postmodernism*:

> The new frontier was the city, where immigrants in massive numbers from Southern and Eastern Europe joined internal migrants driven off the land by the agricultural depression of the 1880s. America was now a continent webbed by railroads and modern communications, with rising urban conglomerates, surging industry, commerce and technology. Towering skyscrapers rose, great department stores appeared, the yellow press spread everywhere. Beneath the general patina of wealth and social aspiration, the massive changes of post-Civil War America were becoming apparent in every walk of life. (221)

Urbanization and increased confidence in the use of machinery that streamlined mass production are among two of the many post-Civil War changes Ruland and Bradbury mention. Early-twentieth-century America sought new ideas, inventions, and theories that would benefit a nation on the rise as both a political and economic power; scientific and technological advancement permeated every aspect of modern American life. As Kenneth Gergen notes, whereas early nineteenth-century America and its arts had revolved around nature and romantic ideals and where love was revered "as intimate communion, intrinsic worth, creative inspiration, moral values, and passionate expression" (27), early-twentieth-century

America set aside romanticism with its "trust in moral values and an ultimate significance to the human endeavor" (27) in favor of empirical science and technology. Gergen further states that "[t]he modernist narrative of progress was not limited to the sciences" (31), claiming that art, literature, and architecture all felt the push of modern progress. Gergen cites renowned architect W.R. Lethargy as "echoing Darwin" in his statement that "'design is a matter of progressive experiment, the working out of a principle by means of adaptation, selection, variation'" (31). Lethargy's positive employment of an evolutionary metaphor in relation to design is acutely optimistic. This optimism illustrates Gillian Beer's explanation of Darwin's popular reception, for "despite its tendency to undermine, the evolutionary metaphor has become also a means of confirming our value, suggesting that we inherit the world at its pinnacle of development and are the bearers of a progressive future" (*Darwin's Plots* 18).

Extending this Darwinian metaphor to include the modern text and its audience helps explain the drastic changes in the production of prose fiction and the form it would take from the late-nineteenth century onward. Like art and architecture, literature was forced to evolve from its early nineteenth-century romantic conventions into a more accurate reflection of the modern era's preoccupation with progress. Where readers of the mid nineteenth-century had devoured the gothic romance of Hawthorne and the transcendental and mystical qualities of Emerson, modern audiences sought material more reflective of their changing times. (While American Realism and Naturalism are two important periods that arise in response to American Romanticism, I will, for the sake of brevity, merely refer to a few texts evocative of those periods). Many late-nineteenth and early-twentieth-century texts catered to the budding capitalist in search of the American dream; articles on "how to get rich quick" were common in early tabloids. While economics played a role in the transformation of literature and tabloid journalism, science played a larger one. Integral to science's role as catalyst for change in literature was a "complex of Darwinian problems that center in the theory of sexual selection and which . . were developed in innumerable variations on the themes of love, courtship, and marriage in the fiction of Howells, James, and their successors" (Bender 315). In his latest book on evolution and literature, *Evolution and "The Sex Problem,"* Bender goes so far as to state that these "successors" or novelists

> read Darwin rather closely, taking from him what they could in efforts to demonstrate their authority as interpreters of the new reality and to engage in the social debate over sexual difference and supposed evolutionary hierarchies according to race, class and culture. (1)

Representative of the increasing incorporation of Darwinian explanation for sexual behavior was Theodore Dreiser's *Sister Carrie*. Explicit in its bleak portrayal of the darker side of the Darwinian reality, *Sister Carrie*

(1902) is one of the most important novels of the early modern era. Although artistically plodding and difficult, Theodore Dreiser's Naturalist novel is an important bridge from the genteel works of the American Realists (such as William Dean Howells and Edith Wharton) to the gritty Modernist prose of Ernest Hemingway.

While problematic for the lengthy editorial commentary of its omniscient narrator, *Sister Carrie* is a vital text when setting the stage for Hemingway's and H.D.'s arrival on the literary scene. *Sister Carrie* is among the first novels in American literature whose female protagonist breaks from culturally constructed codes of morality, puts her own interests ahead of others as well as any notions of right and wrong, and yet still comes out a winner. While initially an impoverished young woman from the country, Dreiser's youthful heroine makes it to the top of society's ladder by "selecting" first Drouet, a budding entrepreneur, and then Hurstwood, a successful married businessman, to make her social and financial ascent. Although initially it appears that Carrie is "led astray" by the handsome Drouet who "carried off with an easy hand" the setting up of Carrie in an apartment (*Sister Carrie* 71), "when it came to the selection," it was really Carrie rather than Drouet who "determined" the sexual situation (*Sister Carrie* 72). When Hurstwood, her married lover, ceases to be of use to her, Carrie's complete abandonment of him results in his financial ruin and suicide. It would appear that Carrie is far more "naturally" suited to the harsh environment of the city than the pathetic Hurstwood, for ultimately it is she who makes the ascent to artistic fame.

Dreiser's implementation of Darwinian language is unmistakable and Carrie's selection, control, and ultimate rejection of Hurstwood exemplifies Darwin's explanation that

> when the females are the selectors, and accept only those males which excite or charm them most, we have reason to believe that it formerly acted on our progenitors. [. . .] for in utterly barbarous tribes the women have more power in choosing, rejecting, and tempting their lovers, or of afterwards changing their husbands, than might have been expected. (*Descent of Man* 901)

It is arguable that Dreiser thought early twentieth-century America not so far removed from Darwin's "barbarous tribes" for Carrie certainly engages in the biologically calculating manner described. Further, her behavior, in light of the Victorian sensibilities of the century just passed, Carrie's behavior while successful, is definitely unexpected. Dreiser appears to consider the behavior of men and women in the early twentieth century to be a tangle of progression and regression. Civilization, he seems to hint, takes a step forward and a step back.

Even as Dreiser presents Carrie as a naturally suited and sexually empowered female, he further complicates her character by giving her artistic talent. In his description of Carrie as artist, Dreiser employs arrestingly

Darwinian language through a secondary character, Ames. Through Ames, Dreiser comments on Carrie's artistic ability, explaining that "there is something about" her "eyes and mouth" that "fits" Carrie for "that sort of work" (*Sister Carrie* 448). Ames tells Carrie he "knows why" she is a "success," for she is the "natural expression of its [the world's] longing," or as he explains, "[t]he world is always struggling to express itself." He implies that the ability to do so has been given her by nature. "Sometimes nature does it in a face-it makes the face representative of all desire" (*Sister Carrie* 448).

First, Ames' comments on Carrie's suitability for stage and song illustrates Darwin's assertions that

> before acquiring the power of expressing their mutual love in articulate language, [Quadrumanous animals] endeavored to charm each other with musical notes and rhythm. So little is known about the use of the voice by the Quadrumana during the season of love, that we have no means of judging whether the habit of singing was first acquired by our male or female ancestors. Women are generally thought to possess sweeter voices than men, and as far as this serves as any guide, we may infer that they first acquired musical powers in order to attract the other sex. (*Descent of Man* 880-81)

If we are to assume that Carrie's ability to sing and act are, in fact, Darwinian propensities intended to make her more desirous to males and therefore, more successful during sexual selection, it could be argued that Hurstwood may have been the first of many sexual "victims." As object of desire and subsequent catalyst for struggle between males, Carrie epitomizes the Darwinian female; she amorally chooses the male most likely to assist her in her struggle for success and survival. While driven by a need to succeed and survive, Carrie is drawn as a simple and relatively sympathetic character. Rather than designed as a "femme fatale," she is portrayed as a product of nature and her behavior is therefore, instinctive. This natural characterization of Carrie is evidence of Dreiser's desire to present human behavior as a response to biological needs. While the text of *Sister Carrie* seems bleak, indeed, it appears that Dreiser was merely replicating what he viewed as the harsh, but natural, reality around him.

The end of the novel is further evidence of Dreiser's Darwinian philosophy as we see the amoral Carrie unhappy but having achieved her dreams of power and financial success. Dreiser's dark realism evinces the growing awareness of Darwin's theory regarding natural selection with its insistent "struggle for existence" as an important influence on human behavior. Carrie's assertive role in the novel is also remarkable evidence of Dreiser's belief in Darwin's theory of sexual selection, which places woman in the role of sexual selector. Even as the resigned Hurstwood lies down with resignation, simultaneously, Carrie mounts the stage in grand success.

Dreiser's honest portrayal of a Darwinian world inadvertently results in one of fiction's most successful female characters.

As both sexual selector and object of desire, Carrie is in control of her life and the life of Hurstwood; however, it would also appear that Carrie is in control of her own body, for while Dreiser's protagonist is a sexually active woman, she neither bears children nor displays any fears of pregnancy. Carrie is driven by impulse and desire to have sex but Dreiser implies that she has no wish for or thought of children. It would appear that Carrie takes the idea of sexual selection a step further than did Darwin. Not only does she select a male with whom to have sex, but she also selects to be childless. This selection can be viewed numerous ways, from incidental and irrelevant to Dreiser's plot to calculatingly progressive on the part of his heroine. At the very least, Carrie's power to choose demonstrates Dreiser's appreciation for evolutionary theory's sexual premises coupled with an awareness of immediate cultural change regarding sex and birth.

Published during the years just preceding the William and Margaret Sanger obscenity trial, Dreiser's novel of 1902 is an acknowledgment of the Sangers' battle for recognition of women's sexuality as the product of innate desire and choice, rather than simply as an instinctive procreational undertaking. Dreiser therefore was complicating Darwin's theories by incorporating ideas of Freud and other sexologists who claimed that sexual repression was responsible for numerous psychological maladies. Engagement in sexual intercourse was increasingly viewed as a "positive" behavior for women and was also being touted as a "cure" for hysteria (Sulloway 249). On a more practical level, Dreiser presumably noted that with the increasing availability of birth control provided by the Sangers and others, women's sexuality would "evolve" to include procreative choice.

For its incorporation of the growing awareness of women's sexuality and desire for control over their lives and bodies, Dreiser's *Sister Carrie* was initially rejected for publication. Once published, *Sister Carrie* was banned in numerous cities in the United States and the release of Dreiser's novel was limited. The publisher's reluctance to advertise *Sister Carrie* is evidence that while America was evolving into a modern society, the acceptance of Darwin's and other sexologists' theories of sexual and natural selection was relative; the war between progress and morality was raging and would often be waged on the pages of America's literature.

Although Dreiser's role as fictional chronicler of a Darwinian world was vastly important to the moderns writers like Hemingway who would come later, his position as newspaper correspondent for many years prior to his career as a novelist is also important when setting the scene for Hemingway's and H.D.'s literary arrival; though his style was verbose, compared to Hemingway's, his plain language and stark description of humanity's ultimate immorality in the face of self-gain was groundbreaking. Although their form was very different, Dreiser and Hemingway would share a desire to construct truthful representations of modern life and their formula for doing so would be honed through their work as newspapermen.

The publication of *Sister Carrie*, while a distinct break from the veiled prose of a century before, was not enough to silence that portion of the population still clinging to Victorian morality. Even as individuals were encouraged to strive for financial success on the one hand, as science and technological progress were topics of discussion in every possible venue, simultaneously, American society was in the throes of an evangelical moral revival which would attack the very essence of modernity. As social activists marched for women's suffrage and birth control in an attempt at improving social conditions, advocates for Anthony Comstock's Society for the Suppression of Vice were attempting to stem the tide of social and sexual change. The moral revival was aided greatly by the rising popularity of presidential hopeful, Woodrow Wilson, whose lively rhetoric was heavily laced with Biblical verse.

Eventually, however, the polarization of American morality would abate, for Comstock's Society membership dwindled quickly after his untimely death in 1915, and many American women were intrigued and relieved at the idea that sex and birth were no longer inextricably bound. As D'Emilio and Freeman state,

> New ideas about sex coincided with a new sense of sexual identity among some Americans. Finally, middle-class cultural radicals, emboldened by the critique of political and economic institutions that left-wing agitators promoted, self-consciously broke with the marital ideals of their upbringing as they sought to construct new forms of personal relationships. All these signs of change pointed toward acceptance of a sexual ethic that encouraged expressiveness. (223)

The social and sexual revolution D'Emilio and Freeman articulate would eventually overpower any lingering Victorian sensibilities, however, and although Americans believed themselves to be the guardians of global morality and democracy, the evolution of sex, as Darwin theorizes it, is a long and complex process which could not be arrested. Interestingly, though the work of Dreiser, Howells, and James at the early part of the century pulls on the threads comprising the fabric of the modern conscience, forcing many Americans to reevaluate religion as explanatory of human existence, the American sense of self had never been richer. However, perhaps the increasing popularity of Spenserian "social Darwinism" is in part responsible for the high self-esteem of many Americans. Coupled with Tom Gibbons's assertions that "evolutionary thinking encouraged various literary critics of the period 1880-1920 to believe in the desirability of an elite social class" (25), the rise in the American sense of self is unsurprising.

The Emergence of Two Moderns

The notion of manifest destiny was also a believable concept to most Americans, and to be American was to occupy the top of the cultural chain. In the light of an idealized American sense of self, we can begin to understand the impact that contemporary biological and psychological theories had on American society as a whole.

Darwin's theory of evolution by means of natural and sexual selection with its instinctive drives to kill and eat and to procreate was perhaps the most influential idea of the late nineteenth and early twentieth century. As Beer points out, everything that preceded Darwin—all thought, scientific, philosophical, moral, and ethical—became questionable. Theories which had once been ideological "givens" were now becoming ideological dinosaurs:

> Everyone found themselves living in a Darwinian world in which old assumptions had ceased to be assumptions, could be at best beliefs or myths, or, at worst, detritus of the past. So the question of who read Darwin or whether a writer had read Darwin, becomes only a fraction of the answer. (*Darwin's Plots* 6)

As Beer implies, evolutionary thought was not confined to the readers of Darwin's books, for although his audience was vast, the books' themes were more so and the texts quickly became topics of conversation everywhere. Bender notes this and explains that "[b]y the 1870s, when virtually every respectable scientist or social thinker was an evolutionist and when all but the aging, committed conservatives like Louis Agassiz perceived Darwin as 'the greatest of prophets,' nearly everyone was to some extent a 'Darwinist'" (*The Descent of Love* 5). As a lay audience became increasingly aware of Darwin's theories, so too did they become versed in the scientific and social theories that sprang up quickly following the publications of his works. Evolutionary theory's popularity as both topic of conversation and "whipping boy" for all that was wrong with society was soon eclipsed by the psychological and sociological theories of Ellis and Freud.

Basing their work on Darwin, both Havelock Ellis and Sigmund Freud created large bodies of work on sexuality and human behavior. Beer explains the importance of Darwin's influence on other fields of study, stating that "[t]he power of Darwin's writing in his culture is best understood when it is seen not as a single origin or 'source,' but in its shifting relations to other areas of study" (*Darwin's Plots* 10). Combined, Darwin, Ellis, and Freud had a profound influence on all of western civilization; it is in modern literature, however, that this influence is particularly evident.

While H.D. did not truly "embrace" Freud until the early '30s and Hemingway decried psychoanalysis completely, Freud's work both dominated and fascinated most of the world for a great part of the first half of this century. It was impossible to produce a text in the modern period without an awareness of psychoanalysis and Freud's "discovery" of the subconscious, as well as his theories of childhood fixations. All had a profound impact on the arts.

Havelock Ellis's work also played its part in forming the philosophies of these writers, and his case studies, particularly those involving female eros, provided examples of sexual fixations that often appear in the texts of both writers. Also important to Hemingway's and H.D.'s sexual representations is Ellis's theory of the metaphysical aspect of human sexuality. Agreeing with Darwin that the sexual drive urging men and women to commingle was instinctive, Ellis further argued that the resulting union rose above this instinctual level and produced something meaningful and near holy between the two.

Rather than imply that one theory of sexuality and human behavior was in and of itself responsible for the philosophical premise behind Hemingway's and H.D.'s work, it is more accurate to state that in varying degrees, the theories of Darwin, Ellis and Freud are all present in their works and further, that all three had a major impact on modern society and its literature. While many individuals in the early twentieth century may not have read Darwin or those scientists who based their work on his findings, it is important to recognize that the ideas presented in his works forever changed the way individuals would view themselves in relation to other individuals and other species.

Published in 1859, *The Origin of Species by Means of Natural Selection* took some time to make its way into the American consciousness. After the initial turmoil over Darwin's book had passed, however, more and more social commentators began to see a link, or more accurately, to create one, between the idea of success and the idea of evolution. This link, as I mentioned above, in the form of Spenserian "social Darwinism" was extremely popular. More specifically, the notion that evolution could be tampered with in order to improve humanity was much discussed, fueled heavily by the unrest an influx of "inferior" races in the form of eastern European immigrants had created among the upper middle class. While Darwin realized that the process of evolution was a natural occurrence which required hundreds of thousands of years, his public audience reinterpreted evolutionary theory, and its misappropriation and misapplication is arguably America's excuse for many of its darkest mistakes in the form of racism, segregation, and misogyny. At the very least, Darwin's work and its subsequent reapplication by his lay audience in tandem with the psychological and social theories which resulted from it helped solidify the invisible social walls separating the affluent, rooted American upper-middle class from the blue-collar, immigrant lower classes. It was in just such a late-nineteenth century, upper-middle class neighborhood that both H.D. and Hemingway grew up.

CHAPTER TWO

Tending the Gardens of Darwin, Ellis and Freud:
The Roots of H.D.'s Sexual Symbols

> I am on the fringes or in the penumbra of the light of my father's science and my mother's art.
> —H.D.

Hilda Doolittle came from an upper-middle class family that could trace its ancestry back for generations. The first of H.D.'s childhood homes was built in the Moravian community of Bethlehem, Pennsylvania. Founded by European Protestant separatists in the 1700's, Bethlehem was a well-developed and successful community of upscale Moravian farmers by 1886, the year of H.D.'s birth. Crucial to the sect's beliefs was the radical notion "that God was the very essence of Love" (Guest 9), an idea reminiscent of Ellis' notions regarding the transcendental nature of sexual relations, as well as the spiritual equality of the sexes, ideas which would play important roles in H.D.'s later life as both woman and writer. In this sheltered and close-knit community, H.D. spent her formative early years. While many of the Moravian cultural habits H.D. acquired would influence her lifelong behavior, they would nevertheless take a back seat to the scientific philosophies espoused by her grandfather, father, and five brothers during her early life. Blending spirituality with evolutionary science is a persistent element of H.D.'s works, and it was no less a part of the major relationships of her life. In the age of evolutionism, H.D. and others like her seemed to have accepted general principles of evolutionary change; she applied these principles to the change, growth, and development occurring in her own life, articulating these changes as a type of personal evolution or transformation, as she does in this letter to daughter Perdita:

> Evolving. Searching. My past, the past, the past that never was, and making something real of it. And it's always eluding me. I think I've found it, and I find it's wrong. But the wrong way can be illuminating too, it so often points out the right way-ultimately. The idea behind the idea is the one I'm really searching for. Again, it's a bit like exploring a galaxy with a trick telescope, picking out pinpoint constellations, and taking optical illusions for their worth, too. And it's all part of the rag-tag-and-bobtail of my sewing basket. Do you follow me? (*Signets* 5)

With this statement, H.D. articulates what would become a lifelong habit: to take an idea and revise it, amend it, add to it, and ultimately recreate it in a philosophical mosaic comprising science, psychology, metaphysics, and myth. The "sewing basket" of her approach to life would at different points be comprised of numerous "spools" or ideas, any one of which would dominate at given times. As Louis Martz points out in his introduction to her collected poems, "[h]er poetry and her prose, like her own psyche, live at the seething junction of opposite forces" (xi). It would take many years and much searching before H.D. would come to terms with her continually shifting self.

Meanwhile, as a child, Hilda would have to settle for existing "on the fringes of" her "father's science or in the penumbra of" her "mother's art." At the age of nine, Hilda and her family moved five miles from Bethlehem to Upper Darby, Pennsylvania, to be close to the Flower Observatory where Charles Doolittle would serve as Professor of Astronomy. Still farm country, Upper Darby was even more prosperous than Bethlehem. The Doolittle home sat on five acres, "an old-fashioned Emersonian American home with an empty, yet productive, countryside surrounding it, and intellectual labors taking place inside" (Guest 16). For H.D., these "intellectual labors" would include reading, studying the stars, like the father she so admired, as well as assisting with "the flower garden capably tended by Mrs. Doolittle" (Guest 17). This time spent with her mother was perhaps more significant than Guest implies for as Friedman asserts, "H.D. identified strongly with her artist mother, but she felt her mother favored her older brother, Gilbert" (*Psyche Reborn* 26). A matriarchal figure, Helen Doolittle hadn't much time for any one child. An accomplished artist and the busy wife of an important professor and mother of five children, Helen was unavailable for much of H.D.'s childhood. As Barbara Guest states of H.D., "[r]eality had handed her a withdrawn father and a mother stranded in domesticity" (17). Only when at work in the flower garden she tended so carefully could Helen be counted on to give the desired attention to the youthful H.D. It is little wonder that garden imagery would play such an integral role in H.D.'s work.

Garden imagery was everywhere in the early twentieth century linking the plant and animal worlds with the world of humans, as scientific theories were carried over into close inspection of human behavior. A particularly acute example of the preoccupation with plants and nature and their analogous relationship with human life was published sometime after Darwin's major works, a book discussing the sexual life of plants by Canadian writer Grant Allen.

Allen's text of 1895, *The Story of the Plants* illustrates how closely the lives of plants mirror the lives of humans. Based almost completely on Darwin's evolutionary theory, Allen's book is organized in chapters which trace the lives of plants through each important phase ("How Plants Eat,"

"How Plants Marry," "Various Marriage Customs," are a few such chapters) and which ultimately attempt to account for the origin of plants and the part they play in the origin of all species. While this small book was hardly widely read, it would have been an extremely likely volume to be found in Charles Doolittle's household, for H.D.'s father spent his life observing nature. As a Professor of Astronomy at the Flower Observatory, he had a preoccupation with "a world of earth and sky" (Guest 15) that was inherited by his only daughter, H.D.

Feeling an outsider as the family's only girl and "second" at the very least in her mother's affections, Hilda desired more of her mother's attention than she received; while this has been critically described as H.D.'s problems with "penis envy" in the past, it seems more accurate to say that the incomplete relationship with her mother caused an early and persistent sense of incompletion in H.D. herself. As she states in *Tribute to Freud*, "[b]ut one can never get near enough, or if one gets near, it is because one has measles or scarlet fever. *If* one could stay near her always, there would be no break in consciousness" (H.D. 33). Seemingly, nearness to her mother provided H.D. with a continuous consciousness or identity that was frequently lacking or interrupted as if she had only fragmentary awareness or was only a portion of herself when alone. It is perhaps this sense of incompleteness that motivated H.D. to search for versions of her mother in her relationships with other women.

While Frances Gregg, H.D.'s first female love, could never be described as "motherly," their intimate relationship, their passionate and tumultuous romance including the shared attentions of Pound, could certainly, for a time, have supplied H.D. with the female attention she so desired. Her later relationship with Winnifred Ellerman (Bryher) who played rescuer and patron, friend and secretary for many years of H.D.'s life is an even better possibility as mother replacement, a possibility H.D. herself entertained. As Friedman points out, "[b]oth Freud and H.D. linked Bryher with Helen Wolle, thereby suggesting that H.D.'s longing for her mother was projected onto her relationship with Bryher" (*Psyche Reborn* 132). Although H.D. rejected the simplistic notion of penis envy as regards her fixation on her mother, she clearly subscribed to some of Freud's ideas; her behavior both as a teenage girl and in her early married life with Richard Aldington displays many of the traits Freud outlines in his discussions of differing types of arrested development. "Many persons," he states, "are detained at each of the stations in the course of development through which the individual must pass; and accordingly, there are persons who never overcome the parental authority and never or very imperfectly, withdraw their affection from their parents" (*The Basic Writings* 618). Even after leaving for Europe in 1911, H.D. would have difficulty with the absence of her mother and to a lesser degree, her father.

Even as H.D.'s mother played a huge role in her relationships with women, so too, would her position as only daughter in a family of boys. Lonely and socially inadept, Hilda desired a sister nearly as much as she did a more nurturing mother. The desire for a sister was compounded by H.D.'s guilt at the death of the sisters her mother had borne but who had died young. "Why is it always a girl who died? Why did Alice die and not Alfred? Why did Edith die and not Gilbert? [...] There was Alice—my own half-sister—Edith, my own sister and I was the third of this trio, these three Fates" (*The Gift* 4). The desire for a sister is inextricably tied to H.D.'s fixation on her mother and would be played out, to some extent, in the relationships with Frances Gregg and other lovers. (Interestingly, the desire for a sister or a "twin self" with whom to share life, and potentially a forbidden love, is actualized by Hemingway and will be discussed later in this work.)

While the time spent in the garden assisting her mother may have had a lasting impact on H.D.'s prose and her persistent linking of gardens to art or artistic endeavor, so too, would the scientific books which occupied the shelves of the family library have a lasting influence on H.D., as would their authors. William Carlos Williams, an early friend and visitor to the Doolittles, would later state that "the spirit of a life of scientific research dominated the household" (Williams, "A Letter," 2-3). Williams' statement is not surprising, for while Hilda's father was Professor of Astronomy, publishing several works in his field (among them, *Practical Astronomy as Applied to Geodesy and Navigation*, 1885), her grandfather was also a scientist and naturalist, the author of *Desmids of the United States* (1884), *Freshwater Algae of the United States*, (1887), and *Diatomaecae of North America* (1890). Introducing H.D. to the flora and fauna of her surrounding Pennsylvania countryside, H.D.'s grandfather inspired in her a deep appreciation for the natural world whose images would inhabit her entire oeuvre.

H.D.'s reading was not restricted to the works of her family, however. She was a voracious and eclectic reader, a habit she never outgrew, although her college career at Bryn Mawr was cut short, "interrupted by her stormy engagement to Ezra Pound" (Robinson 11). In her final days at Bryn Mawr, H.D. was "awakened" (Guest 22) to Greek drama in the form of Euripedes' "Iphegenia in Aulis." The works of Euripedes would play a major role in H.D.'s life, as she first translated and then later emulated them in many of her Imagist poems, including her own version of "Iphegenia in Aulis." Ezra Pound would also play a primary role in Hilda's continuing education at home, introducing Hilda to numerous works including those of Swedenborg and Freud, as well as to the classic and Renaissance poets. "Hilda diligently studied Latin, Greek and the classics," states biographer Janice Robinson, and "she and Pound read Rosetti and the Pre-Raphaelites" (11). The texts he gave her to read, like Pound himself, would influence H.D. and her work dramatically.

Out of the curious blending of scientific and romantic reading of these early years, H.D.'s own artistic form emerged. The initial Imagist poems, "Priapus" and "Hermes of the Ways" are acute examples of this blending, for these first two poems although distinctly Greek in style, are emphatically Freudian in their symbology. As Janice Robinson points out in her discussion of "Priapus," "no esoteric Freudian understanding is required to grasp the image presented in the title of this poem; Priapus or *priapos* is the Greek word for the male genital organ personified as a God" (30). Whether H.D. focused this early artistic endeavor on male genitalia due to the persistent importance of men in her life and her subsequent feelings of marginalization because of their preponderance or not, at the very least, one can assert that her subject was a peculiar one for a young woman of her day. The phallic imagery in this early work resounds again later in poems such as "Mid-day" where in one stanza, H.D. deifies a tree:

> O poplar, you are great
> among the hill stones,
> while I perish on the path
> among the crevices of rocks. (*Collected Poems* 10)

and even more overtly in "Pear Tree," which is worthy of reproducing in its entirety here:

> Silver dust
> lifted from the earth,
> higher than my arms reach,
> you have mounted.
> O silver,
> higher than my arms reach,
> you front us with great mass;
> no flower ever opened
> so staunch a white leaf,
> no flower ever parted silver
> from such rare silver;
> O white pear,
> your flower-tufts
> thick on the branch
> bring summer and ripe fruits
> in their purple hearts. (*Collected Poems* 39)

However, the peculiarity of H.D.'s subject matter seems less so if we place her work in the context of her reading of the romantics. As Cassandra Laity argues, "H.D.'s transformed romanticism drew upon the romantics' preoccupation with the split between eros and spirituality projected in the dialectical landscapes of romantic quest romance"

("H.D.'s Romantic Landscapes: The Politics of the Garden" *Signets* 111). Laity further asserts that even as H.D. employs a rubric created by the romantics, she offers a revised version of it by shifting the romantic questor's gaze from male to female. "Shifting the focus of romantic quest to the female imagination, H.D. revised the tradition," suggests Laity, "to create a poetics of female desire which both used and critiqued the conventions of romanticism" ("H.D.'s Romantic Landscapes" 111).

Laity's articulation of the romantic revision at work in H.D.'s poetry provides interesting insight into the artistic maneuvering she accomplished even in her earliest works. The audacity H.D. displayed in employing and revising the romantic quest formula is an early glimpse at her ability and willingness to borrow, modify, and ultimately transform an existing artistic form. More importantly, Laity's interpretation of H.D.'s employment of the romantic quest helps explain why the symbols the poet employed were dually gendered. Whereas the male romantics described a quest that would result in the capture of the female, resulting in her subjugation by male questor,

> H.D. found affirmation for her exploration of same-sex love in the more homoerotic emphasis of decadents such as Swinburne, she forged her own poetics of desire from the Victorian-romantics, redeeming 'forbidden sexuality from its place in the appropriately decadent' lower paradise to create a triumphant myth of female visionary and erotic power. ("H.D.'s Romantic Landscapes" 112)

While Laity's discussion provides extraordinary insight into H.D.'s employment of erotic imagery, no less helpful in an analysis of her poetics is the increasingly "mainstream" discussion of Freudian theory. Just as Darwin's work became part of the cultural landscape of the late nineteenth and early twentieth century, so too, did Freud and other sexologists like Fleiss and to a lesser degree, Kraft-Ebing. If we were to accept that Freud's works became part of mainstream language and culture almost immediately following their publication, it would follow that H.D. was well aware of her employment of phallic imagery. Freud describes this imagery as consisting of "[a]ll elongated objects, sticks, tree-trunks, umbrellas (on account of the opening, which might be likened to an erection), all sharp and elongated weapons, knives, daggers, and pikes" (*The Basic Writings* 371). The employment of these images so early in her poetic career are testimony to the impact H.D.'s reading of scientific and sexual theories had on her artistic efforts. It would seem that her growing awareness of sex and sexuality was woven almost immediately into her texts. As many critics assert that even H.D.'s imagist poetics contain references to her life and sexuality, it would seem unsurprising that at a point so crucial to her sexual development (engaging in romantic liaisons with both Pound and Gregg), H.D. would employ imagery so suggestive of genitalia. The persistent linking of flowers and other plants with actual people in H.D.'s life, particularly those with whom she was sexually or romantically involved, is particularly prevalent in her "Sea Garden" poems such as those noted above. And seemingly, just as her life reflected a sexual ambiguity, so did her poetics, for as persistent as the presence of the phallus is the recurring imagery of the vagina as represented by flowers, and a blending of both images is contained in "Pear Tree."

Although H.D. decried Freud's description of her neurosis as being in part due to penis envy or desire for exclusive attention from her mother as in a case of arrested development, it is difficult to deny Freud completely because of the strong associative ties flowers had to her mother, the "original" sex object in H.D.'s life, and to all others with whom H.D. would be sexually linked. According to Freud, H.D. had "spent her life searching for her mother" (Letter from Freud to H.D., 1934). To some degree, it would appear he was correct.

In her prose works, flowers would be linked with every important woman in H.D.'s life. While one cannot be certain that the persistent linking of women and flowers in her prose and poetry sprang from H.D.'s childhood experience tending her mother's flower garden and the fond associations related to this experience, it is an intriguing idea when considered in light of Freud's analysis articulated above. The huge role of flower imagery in the early works of H.D., and the persistent linking of flowers with women, is fascinating both for its Freudian (and Darwinian) implications. More specifically, in his explanation of dream symbols, Freud describes symbols of male and female genitalia both exactly and generally (the most specific articulations being, of course, of the male organs—one of many examples of the patriarchal preferences in Freud's work). While male genitalia is basically represented by anything long or powerful, as explained above, female genitalia is often represented by

> [s]mall boxes, chests, cupboards, and ovens correspond to the female organ; also cavities, ships, and all kinds of vessels.—A room in a dream generally represents a woman; the description of its various entrances and exits is scarcely calculated to make us doubt this interpretation. (*Basic Writings* 371)

Flowers, according to the psychoanalyst, fit this general description, as they are often "open and cavernous" and he provides several case studies of flower imagery in dreams as representative of sexual feelings. However, as flowers organically contain male *and* female genitalia, persistent flower imagery could represent an inherently bisexual affiliation or sexual ambiguity. Further, symbolic imagery regarding sexuality or sexual performance and behavior is not relegated solely to dreams. As Freud explains,

> [t]he preoccupation of the imagination with one's own body is by no means peculiar to or characteristic of the dream alone. My analyses have shown me that it is constantly found in the unconscious thinking of neurotics, and may be traced back to sexual curiosity, whose object,

in the adolescent youth or maiden, is the genitals of the opposite sex, or even of the same sex. (*Basic Writings* 366)

While it would appear, then, that H.D.'s use of garden imagery, flowers in particular, could, indeed, articulate her preoccupation with and interest in her sexuality and the sexuality of other men and women in her life (and no one appears to dispute this), her employment of these symbols may also have indicated a choice to hide from the ultimate deciphering or "decoding" which could have led to a concrete articulation of her particular sexuality and a release from her sexual fixations. Freud asserts that while plants and flowers do, in fact, suit as representations of sexuality, they can also indicate a choice to hide from one's sexuality. He states that

> the groups of ideas appertaining to plant-life, or to the kitchen, are just as often chosen to conceal sexual images; in respect of the former everyday language, the sediment of imaginative comparisons dating from the remotest times, has abundantly paved the way (the 'vineyard' of the Lord, the 'seed' of Abraham, the 'garden' of the maiden in the Song of Songs). (*Basic Writings* 366)

Seemingly, even as H.D. sought images evocative of her sexuality and implemented these images into her poetics, she appears to negate any substantive analysis of her specific sexual orientation. As preoccupied as she is with sexually loaded imagery, her search for a complete and authentic self seems to be a search outside or beyond the boundaries of articulated sexuality. Her position as sexually ambiguous or "nebulous" was not disturbed even after her lengthy bouts of psychoanalysis. This is confirmed by the near absence of any mention of sexuality (beyond the mother fixation discussed earlier) in her notes documenting her sessions with Freud. The resistance H.D. demonstrates to being sexually categorized was shared by other female moderns such as Bryher who often displayed a deep and abiding affection for men even while maintaining lifelong intimate relationships with women. Although today we would most certainly define these women as bisexuals, and indeed, Freud's (and Darwin's before him) assertion that all creatures are inherently bisexual would initially prove "liberating" (Friedman *Psyche Reborn* 129), they would resist even this category in favor of a sexuality undefined or oppositional; rather than *bisexual,* a half-life of each sex, H.D. and others like her seemed to be either heterosexual or homosexual at *any given point*. While the difference may seem semantic, it is the difference between *duality* and *polarity*. Barbara Guest describes H.D. in this manner in her paradoxically titled biography of H.D., *Herself Defined*. According to Guest, H.D. "could be seen either as a Greek maiden or a Greek god. Hermes or Aphrodite; Artemis, especially" (33). As Freud himself often described H.D. as suffering from narcissism, these godlike identities seem appropriate, both for their sexual polarity and for their grandeur. However, as I pointed out earlier, H.D. and Freud were often at odds and their differences would at times be very great. While

H.D. denied much of what Freud applied with regards to her particular neurosis, she also hotly debated with him on points of artistic merit, the usefulness of science, and the mental abilities of women. Susan Friedman claims that many of the moderns had difficulties with Freud's theories and asserts that

> [i]n order for Freud's ideas to act as catalyst, H.D. and her fellow artists in the modernist tradition had to leave him far behind in the dust of his imagined empiricism. His materialist conception of reality and the resulting negative valuation of psychical realities had to be rejected if his rich insights into nonrational thought processes were to have an impact on art. (*Psyche Reborn* 97)

Friedman's insistence that H.D. and other moderns had to first embrace Freud's ideas of the unconscious and then reject his ideas of materialism and empiricism is an effective way of understanding H.D.'s employment of and reaction against both Darwinian and Freudian theories. For a time, the reaction against Freud would result in a movement toward his contemporary, Havelock Ellis. Indeed, it would be Ellis' description of sexual inversion that would inform modern texts such as Radclyffe Hall's *The Well of Loneliness* and Bryher's *Two Selves* (Friedman *Psyche Reborn* 129).

Ellis' presentation of sexual inversion argues for its close association with power and intelligence. In his *Studies in the Psychology of Sex,* Ellis describes sexual inversion

> to be accompanied by high intellectual ability in a woman as in a man. The importance of a clear conception of inversion is indeed in some respects, under present social conditions, really even greater in the case of women than of men. for if, as has sometimes been said of our civilization, 'this is a man's world,' the large proportion of able women inverts, whose masculine qualities render it comparatively easy for them to adopt masculine avocations, becomes a highly significant fact. (1:4 196)

Underlying Ellis' statement is his employment of Darwin's articulation first, of the superiority of the male mind and second, that because to some degree, female inverts possess an inherently greater portion of masculine attributes than do "normal" women, it is likely they will possess greater intelligence. Ellis' notion of inversion was far preferable to Freud's description of the homosexual, so much so that numerous modern writers and artists were quite willing to associate themselves with Ellis' theory. The inherently "biological" trap of inversion vindicated the feelings of many lesbian and bisexual moderns and although she later rejected his inversional premise, H.D. undertook a relationship with Ellis that would last for many years.

Like her sexuality, H.D.'s positioning with scientific and sexologic theories would often be a polarity wherein she would seemingly swing from side to side as the theories suited her. Seemingly, the "sewing basket" philosophy H.D. described to Perdita resulted in her ability to tailor theories and their language to suit her purpose, employing and rejecting them as she saw fit with no apparent unease.

CHAPTER THREE

Matricidal Tendencies:
Hemingway's Battle Begins

> Art and science contended for mastery in the new house on Kenilworth Avenue.
> —-Carlos Baker

Like H.D.'s, Hemingway's early upbringing was a curious blending of religion, art, and science. "Rigorous" Christians both, Hemingway's mother and father had strong ideas about morality, duty, familial obedience, and marriage. However, these Christian ideals were illustrated in the Hemingway household far more pragmatically than spiritually. While there is no doubt that Grace and Clarence Hemingway were spiritual "believers" in a Christian God, neither of them appears to have pondered their religion too deeply nor to have engaged in any overt exhibitions of religious or spiritual fervor. Instead, the Hemingway's approach to Christianity was active engagement in habits that built strong bodies and good health. A good Christian was a healthy Christian. In keeping with this, both parents were strong believers in work, self-discipline, temperance, and exercise as vital elements of Christian behavior. This exercise was generally undertaken in the woods and on the water at Lake Walloon, the site of the family vacation home.

An "outdoorsy" family, the Hemingway clan spent a great deal of time fishing, boating, swimming, and collecting Indian artifacts. In his first five years of life, a great deal of which was spent at Lake Walloon, Hemingway would learn about and quickly grow to love the natural world under the tutelage of father Clarence who himself had a strong preoccupation with the outdoors. Biographer Kenneth Lynn describes the elder Hemingway as "[a] marvelous marksman with both shotgun and rifle, an accomplished fisherman, a master of every technique for surviving in a wilderness, Dr. Hemingway was the complete woodsman" (*Hemingway* 35). Clarence Hemingway was no easy act to follow, and it is apparent that Hemingway's preoccupation with all things "masculine" is the result of his capable father. Competing with such a father would prove to be both challenging and ultimately fatal, for Ernest Hemingway's complex and often disappointing relationship with Clarence would provide much grist for the author to grind and no event in Hemingway's life was more profound than his father's suicide.

The Nick Adams stories are often romanticized experiences the two Hemingways shared as the young Nick accompanies the respected doctor on outings which teach him many things about nature and often, human behavior. In the stories, both Nick and his father appear idealized versions of the Hemingways as the doctor is seemingly all-knowing and capable while the boy Nick is endlessly curious and wise beyond his years. With "Indian Camp" for example, Hemingway has Nick accompany his doctor-father while he tends to a woman in childbirth. "Inside on a wooden bunk lay a young Indian woman. She had been trying to have her baby for two days" (*The Short Stories* 92). Although the 48-hour labor obviously implies that something is drastically wrong, the doctor says simply to Nick that "[t]his lady is going to have a baby" (92). Like his father, Nick stays calm and watches the process of the ensuing Caesarean section with no qualms; even when the worry over his wife grows so great that the Indian father in the story slits his own throat, the young boy displays only "excitement." Seemingly, even in his fiction, Hemingway was proving to his father that on some level, he could "keep up." This idea takes on greater import and poignancy when one contemplates a passage excised from "Indian Camp" which portrays Nick as less than brave. Instead, the passage begins, "[h]e was always a little frightened of the woods at night."

Whether or not Hemingway was aware of the intense and consistent competition he had with his father, the author's persistent desire for paternal approval while simultaneously disdaining much of his father's behavior seems a classic example of Freud's articulation of the Oedipal complex (for which the grown Hemingway would express much disdain). Indeed, his unawareness of an Oedipal conflict makes much sense as one analyzes Hemingway's fictional father-figures for they are a puzzling combination of admiration, disgust, and self-identification. Freud's articulation of the Oedipal conflict is worthy of lengthy elaboration here. He states that

> [i]t may be that we were all destined to direct our first sexual impulses toward our mothers, and our first impulses of hatred and violence toward our fathers; our dreams convince us that we were. King Oedipus, who slew his father Laius and wedded his mother Jocasta, is nothing more or less than a wish-fulfilment—the fulfilment of the wish of our childhood. But we, more fortunate than he, in so far as we have not become psychoneurotics, have since our childhood succeeded in withdrawing our sexual impulses from our mothers and in forgetting our jealousy of our fathers. (*Basic Writings* 308)

In keeping with Freud's explanation of the Oedipal complex, not all the fictionalized versions of the senior Hemingway are as flattering as the portrayal in "Indian Camp." "The Doctor and the Doctor's Wife" illustrates the author's unhappiness at what he felt was his father's emasculation by

Grace Hemingway and his desire for the doctor to do something about it, even if it meant using a gun. In the story, the doctor employs two Indians to cut up some logs that have fallen off a steamer so that he can burn them as firewood. Initially, this is problematic because it displays a dishonesty in the doctor, i.e., taking something that doesn't belong to him. When the Indians joke about the doctor's "stolen" wood, he denies the theft defensively and begins to threaten them. "If you call me Doc once again, I'll knock your eye teeth down your throat" (*The Short Stories* 101).

After the Indians and the doctor engage in a brief but heated argument, the Indians walk off laughing and the doctor enters his cottage, chagrined. His wife, hearing him enter, asks, "Aren't you going back to work, dear?" Annoyed both at the situation and at his questioning wife, the doctor shouts, "No!" When he is forced by her to explain what happened, the doctor must also be subjected to Bible phrases and platitudes well memorized for just such moments as these.

The story ultimately ends with the doctor putting away his shotgun and joining Nick to hunt for squirrels. The story is fascinating for how much it reveals about Hemingway's feelings about his father, his mother, and his father's suicide. Closely read, Nick's appearance at the end of the story acts as a tonic on the doctor, as if fulfilling some wish on Hemingway's part that rather than use the shotgun on himself, Clarence would have put it aside and joined his son, therefore negating the need for suicide. Indeed, the father-figure in several Hemingway stories is distracted from self-harm either by Nick or some other youthful character.

Hemingway's mixed and incomplete emotions regarding his father are similar to those felt by H.D. towards her mother; seemingly when not with "the preferred parent," one or the other of them was not "whole." Hemingway's fixation on and competition with Clarence also demonstrates a sense of the arrested development experienced by H.D. Intriguingly, the similarities do not end there for just as H.D. was an only girl in a family of men, for much of his life, Hemingway was the only boy in a family of women. Not until age fifteen was second son Leicester born and as Baker points out, "he had come too late to be the companion that Ernest had long desired" (*Ernest Hemingway: A Life Story* 19).

Due perhaps to his often rich but strange relationship with his father, Hemingway expressed both love for and antipathy towards his mother. Freud comments on the love-hate relationship with parents and states that "[f]alling in love with one parent and hating the other forms part of the permanent stock of the psychic impulses which arise in early childhood" (*Basic Writings* 306). In the case of Hemingway, it is difficult to truly conclude with which parent he may have "been in love" as his relationships with both were so bipolar. However, one thing is clear: as the domineering matriarch of the family, Grace would forever be a thorn in Hemingway's side. In part, his skewed maternal affections were clearly a result of Grace's ultimate domination over her husband; perhaps Hemingway feared that she would ultimately "castrate" or emasculate him, as well. This point will be discussed at length in a later chapter. It should be noted here, however, that Hemingway's relationship with his parents in later youth and adulthood would ever be strained.

Much of the emotional tension between Hemingway and his parents could have resulted from his peculiar upbringing, for while the Hemingway parents would appear to be ideal and loving ones, they would often allow, indeed encourage, behavior among the Hemingway siblings that bordered on the peculiar, much of it associated with the outdoorsy lifestyle mentioned above. Lynn states as much when he describes the family swims taken on Lake Walloon:

> Once Dr. Hemingway started teaching Marcelline and Ernest to swim, he ordered both children to put on bathing suits. Still, on certain evenings he allowed them to take a goodnight dip in the nude. This privilege was soon extended to Ursula and Sunny as well, and then to Carol. Even in his teens, Ernest and his sisters went swimming in the dark without suits. It made all of us feel, Marcelline said later, like members of a "Secret Society." (*Hemingway* 54)

While swimming naked with siblings seems innocent enough as children, the idea of Hemingway doing so as a teenager presents the possibility that while it might have seemed natural enough, he may have felt some sense of underlying shame at this behavior or if not, perhaps some underlying guilt at his *failure to do so*. At the very least, engagement in this activity with his youthful sisters must have, on some level, seemed titillating to the young Hemingway; the very real idea of sexual interest between siblings seems even evident particularly when one considers his fictional representation of his relationship with sister Ursula, specifically in "The Last Good Country" in which Ursula (called "Littless" in the tale) announces that she wishes to be Nick's "common law wife" and "have a couple of children." These comments, coupled with the kissing and the escape in the story (which reads markedly like an elopement) are unmistakably sexual. It is apparent that while there is certainly no proof or reason to imply that Hemingway acted on any underlying sexual attractions toward his female siblings, the attraction was there and he was well-aware of it. This attraction must certainly have crossed his mind when reading Darwin, Freud, and Ellis who all articulate incest as the one great cultural taboo. It could also figure in very strongly to Hemingway's lifelong attraction to women with rather "boyish" appearances, for Hemingway frequently asserted that another sister, Carol, "looked as a girl exactly as" Hemingway had "as a boy" (Lynn 54). Gender here seems curiously blended as does attraction, for even while Carol looks like Hem as a boy, she is also according to him "the most beautiful" girl. Boy, girl, attraction, siblings, twinning—all are knotted inextricably in Hemingway's early life and these ties were never unravelled. They become elements of Hemingway's fiction and inform the creation of all his greatest characters, coming to rest, finally, in his most intense "gender exploration" in *The Garden of Eden*.

While swimming was perhaps the most interesting activity the Hemingway siblings undertook as a group under the watchful eye of their father, it was by no means the only one. Walking in the woods was also a near-daily occupation while staying at Lake Walloon. As a doctor, Clarence Hemingway's attraction to the natural world was often illustrated very scientifically. With his children, Clarence would name much of the flora and fauna they witnessed. Not content to simply observe the life around him, however, Clarence took to taxidermy as a means of preserving and scrutinizing local wildlife. In a similar vein, he collected a huge number of Pottowani Indian artifacts that he meticulously examined and catalogued. There is little doubt that these scientific and anthropologic endeavors influenced the youthful Hemingway, particularly when Grace describes three-year-old Ernest as "a natural scientist, loving everything in the way of bugs, stones, shells, birds, animals, insects, and blossoms" in her daily journal. It is interesting to note that while the young Hemingway would spend endless hours patiently observing wildlife, tireless when walking, boating, or fishing, he would have little patience when in the evening the family was gathered to say their prayers. After a few words, Hemingway would terminate his participation in this activity by declaring, "Amen," and running out of the room. Apparently the interest in God with particular regard to Catholicism which Hemingway developed in later life was absent in his youth.

Just as scientific endeavors were closely linked to Christian behavior in the Hemingway family, so too, were the arts; for Grace Hemingway, frustrated opera diva and amateur painter, the arts represented an integral part of daily life. Her great appreciation for music and other forms of art played a huge role in Grace's childrearing; not content to simply teach her children an appreciation for God and nature, Grace was insistent that they should also acquire a taste and aptitude for some form of artistic creativity. Carlos Baker notes that "[h]er own deep-dyed belief in creativity made her long to develop the talents of her children to the highest possible degree" (9). To achieve this desire, Grace would take great pains, and a great deal of the family income, in designing a home that would have at its center, a music room. While frequently used as a schoolroom for her voice and piano pupils, Grace also insisted that each of the Hemingway children have music lessons there, as well. Grace Hemingway's musical aptitude and appreciation bear striking resemblance to similar characteristics in Helen Doolittle and the linking of artistic creativity to their mothers is a trait Hemingway and H.D. shared. The maternal affiliation with creativity is perhaps one of the most complicated and important biographical and aesthetic similarities between the two authors for it would be these matriarchs who would dominate both their personal and artistic lives.

The home that Grace helped design was located in Oak Park, Illinois, an exclusive suburb that boasted the Frank Lloyd-Wrights as neighbors. Carlos Baker describes the Hemingway household as one in which "[a]rt and science contended for mastery" (8), a description reminiscent of the sentiments expressed by William Carlos Williams regarding the home of H.D. Even as "art contended with science," so too, did Grace contend with Clarence; the household on Kenilworth Avenue was often noisy with disagreements between the two, and many of these disagreements would involve childrearing. All too frequently, Clarence, weary with arguing, would give in to the more adamant and long-winded Grace; while happy to take on many of the domestic chores which Grace abhorred and which Clarence felt were for him "hobbies," he was not happy with Grace's tendency to "feminize" the young Ernest. Unhappy though he was regarding this behavior, Clarence could not bring himself to stand his ground. As a result, it was here in suburbia that, as Spilka points out, Hemingway's "quarrel with androgyny" began.

Worth noting here is Hemingway's observation of his father's frequent occupation of a nontraditional gender role; Clarence's apparent comfort in doing so must have left a lasting impression on Hemingway for even as his mother was insisting, indeed forcing, Ernest to display himself in nontraditional garb, he was witnessing a willing occupation of nontraditional gender activity. Perhaps his father's apparently unquestionable masculinity as displayed by his abilities to shoot, fish, box and any number of other "manly" occupations inspired Hemingway with an appreciation for men who could "do" things "like a man", even if those things were normally associated with women. This makes some sense when one examines the numerous pejorative remarks Hemingway made regarding homosexuals for nearly all of them refer to dress and "mincing" behavior (which appears to relate directly back to his experience as a child). Scott Donaldson addresses Hemingway's detestation of homosexuals as being lifelong and virulent. Donaldson asserts that Hemingway's

> Oak Park upbringing had not prepared him for sexual arrangements overtly practiced in other parts of the world. From Europe in the early 1920s, he gossiped relentlessly on the topic. Readers of the *Toronto Star Weekly*, for example, read about 'utterly charming young men, with rolling white sweaters and smoothly brushed hair,' who wintered in the best hotels in Switzerland on the proceeds from their bridge games 'with women who are old enough to be their mothers and who deal the cards with a flashing of platinum rings on plump fingers.' (*By Force of Will* 182)

Hemingway couldn't tolerate the affected behavior he felt was continually exhibited by "queers" but as Donaldson points out, his consistent condemnation of homosexual behavior bordered on mania. This great antipathy has been much discussed, often as a potential ruse to hide what has been presented as Hemingway's own latent homosexual tendencies. However, what is seldom presented is any reason *for* those latent tendencies; here I argue that Hemingway's extreme responses to homosexuals and their behavior is caused by a fear that is twofold. First, the emasculation or psychological castration of his father at the hands of his mother which Hemingway witnessed as a child left a deep and lasting impact on Hemingway's sexuality and attendant sexual phobias with particular regard to homosexuality. Possibly, Hemingway feared that emasculation by a woman as a form of homosexuality and subsequent loss of virility along with loss of the phallus which is its center. However, while the emasculation of his father most certainly informed Hemingway's fears regarding phallic loss and homosexuality, so too, did his experiences on Lake Walloon. Kenneth Lynn describes the author's castration complex as potentially arising from Hemingway's seeing sister Marcelline (with whom he was "twinned" by Grace) naked.

> Did the infant boy take pride in the equipment that set him apart from Marcelline? Or did the sight of her smoothness make him think that she had suffered some sort of dreadful accident which might soon befall him as well? or were pride and fear intermingled in his turbulent imagination? Familiar Freudian speculations these, which acquire extra force in this case because Ernest would soon become aware that he and Marcelline were being treated like twins of the same sex. And in years to come, the horrific image of phallic loss would be made light of by Hemingway in tall-tale jokes about such matters as the hazards of skiing in subzero temperatures, and dealt with seriously in two anguishing works of fiction. (*Hemingway* 53)

Hemingway's horror of homosexuals probably did arise out of fears of castration and emasculation created in childhood. Notably, one of Hemingway's few documented fistfights resulted from an accusation that his masculinity was somewhat questionable. Scott Donaldson describes this fistfight as a response to Max Eastman's suggestion that like "[m]ost of us too delicately organized babies who grow up to be artists" Hemingway would "suffer at times from that small inward doubt" (Donaldson 186). Hemingway's doubts regarding his masculinity, his fears of castration and emasculation were years in the making; their accompanying hostility while certainly in no way condonable does appear, to some degree, understandable. To simply label Hemingway as "homophobic" or "latent" is as inaccurate as similar labels describing him as misogynistic. Such labels are oversimplifications of much deeper and far more compelling issues.

Hemingway's detestation of homosexuals conflicts sharply with his seeming appreciation for androgyny and willing exploration of gender traits and behavior. This paradox, however, is the nexus of the author's sexuality and creativity. Because of his experiences as a child which resulted in an acute Oedipal fixation, an intense fear of castration, and a preoccupation with androgyny, Hemingway's sexuality was a morass of conflict and confusion. However, the mixed emotions and desires would act as catalysts for writing, writing which would be informed not just by experience but by the theories of sexuality occupying the very air of the twentieth-century. And like H.D.'s, Hemingway's sexuality seemed to consist of two opposing poles, either of which could be in the ascendant at any given point manifesting itself in the characters peopling his fictional worlds.

Those characters displaying androgynous characteristics are most likely the result of Hemingway's peculiar early relationship with sister, Marcelline. Although eighteen months separated the birth of Ernest and Marcelline Hemingway, from the time Grace Hemingway gave birth to Ernest, she insisted on "twinning" Ernest and sister Marcelline, dressing them alike, giving them similar haircuts, and introducing them as her precious "twin girls." Grace took this twinship quite seriously for a number of years, not allowing Ernest to sport a boy's haircut until nearly age seven. At this point, she also finally ceased her attempts at dressing Ernest and his sister alike, but insisted on keeping Marcelline back in school twice so that she would occupy the same grade as her younger brother. The idea of hair, hair color, haircuts, hair dying, and hair length become, presumably as a result of Hemingway's prolonged "girlish" hairdo, integral to Hemingway's description of women both in his fiction and in his life. Considering the import of hair as a secondary sex characteristic in the work of Darwin and as an object of sexual fixation in the works of Ellis and Freud, this is a point well worth noting and one which will be taken up in a later chapter.

While Ernest and Marcelline were perhaps the most acutely affected by Grace's attempts at "androgynizing" her children, the remaining Hemingway siblings were also raised androgynously, all eventually taught to shoot, ride, and box as well as cook and sew. Compounded with the insistence on teaching their children the roles occupied by both men and women, Grace and Clarence Hemingway also insisted that the children be exposed to both genteel and frontier or pioneering activities. Mark Spilka insists that the blending of traditionally male and female traits with class-crossing experiences left a profound impact on Hemingway, maintaining that such a non-traditional and androgynous upbringing caused Ernest to suffer confusion and frustration (as I argue above). Spilka states that

> [h]is portraits of sportsmen and soldiers, rum runners and runaways, were part of a last-ditch attempt to revive the lost frontier and the possibilities of male self-definition it seemed to offer. The attempt went hand in hand, moreover, with his suppression of the rival female emphasis on manly strength and tenderness in his childhood, a suppression that seems all too clear in his satiric portraits of genteel Christian mothers. He could not admit to the "softening feminine influence" that had helped to shape his manliness. (63)

The suppression which Spilka refers to became evident in Hemingway's behavior when as a teenager, he realized for the first time his father's "degrading subservience" to Grace, which resulted in much "loss of respect" for Clarence and fear for his own masculinity (Lynn 63). It is in these teenage years that Hemingway began to lose affection for the mother to whom he had once felt so closely drawn. As a result of this loss of affection, the teenage Hemingway began to resist Grace's interfering mothering and to resent his father's "disciplinarianism" (Lynn 63). The combination of Grace and Clarence Hall's dominating parenting resulted in Hemingway's emotional withdrawal and determination to remove himself from his parents' control. Kenneth Lynn notes that this withdrawal was "particularly noticeable during the vacation months in Michigan" when in years "1915, 1916, and 1917 he slept most nights in a tent behind Windemere" (the family vacation home) "or in another tent across the lake at Longfield Farm, or in a camp he established for himself at Murphy's Point" (Lynn 64). After these tentative steps at "leaving" home, Hemingway actually departed Oak Park in 1917, taking a job with the Kansas City *Star*.

Even though his move to Kansas City and eventual journey to the European front resulted partly from his desire to remove himself from his mother's influence, the miles between Oak Park and Rome did nothing to rid Hemingway of his mother, for as Kenneth Lynn explains, "[a]lthough he had reached the point of wanting to break completely free of her, he would not be able to bring it off, nor would he be able to do so in future years, not even after he had all but ceased to write to her. All his life, his mother would remain the dark queen of Hemingway's inner world" (65).

As with H.D.'s mother, Hemingway's "dark queen" would influence his writing and personal life; spending most of his adulthood putting physical and emotional distance between Grace and himself, Hemingway would nevertheless relentlessly reproduce "mother figures" in numerous works of short fiction. The inability to completely sever the mother/child bond is an important link between Hemingway and H.D. which I will revisit in later chapters. At this point, it is sufficient to know that both were compelled to leave home and escape maternal bonds. While H.D. left for Europe in 1911 under the guise of a summer vacation, once there, she vowed that in Europe she would stay. Although joined by her parents in August of that year, H.D. convinced them to allow her to remain in England; she would not return to the United States for nearly a decade.

Hemingway also departed America eagerly, filled as he was with illusions of heroic acts like those outlined in Horace Walpole's *The Dark Forest*, "a war story grounded in firsthand experience" (Lynn 66). Spending the year immediately following graduation from high school working as a reporter for the Kansas City *Star*, Hemingway covered "hospital stories" in his desire to witness the violence of the Kansas City crime scene. Perhaps in another attempt at seeing action up close, Hemingway joined the ambulance corps in 1918 and arrived in Rome June 6 of that year. Remarkably, Hemingway went from riding in the back of ambulances to driving them. These first ventures into lands unknown would begin a pattern of expatriation for both H.D. and Hemingway, caught up as they were in an endless search for meaning and identity.

CHAPTER FOUR

Foreigner at Home and Abroad

> Who gave me this broken duality? Who gave me this curse of intimate perception?
> —H.D.

Barbara Guest explains H.D.'s departure for Europe as a response to her unfinished romance with Ezra Pound and her increasing dependence on Frances Gregg. Emotionally attached to them both, H.D. was undecided on what to do, so following Ezra to Europe in the company of Gregg seemed her most promising option. Guest describes the complicated state of affairs between the three as compounded by Pound's burgeoning popularity in England and his desire to become a world talent. "He wished an international reputation," states Guest, and therefore "[h]e had no time for Hilda" (25). When not preparing poems for his upcoming return trip to Europe, however, Pound would "take an almost obsessive interest in Hilda" (25). This "hot and cold" treatment by Pound was both distressing and perplexing, for although H.D. was in love with Frances Gregg, she was also intellectually and emotionally tied to Pound and by all accounts, not ready to lose him to European society and success. Her fiancé and mentor, Pound was also H.D.'s major artistic and intellectual connection. While she had experienced "losing" him temporarily on his jaunts to Europe, he had returned and, albeit sporadically, visited her at her parents' home, bringing with him his latest ideas on art and thought. The idea of Pound moving on to world success and departing her life forever was too much to bear; for H.D., this must only be a temporary parting. Guest explains that H.D. "intuited" Pound's recurring presence in her life: "Yet he had returned to her, had he not? True, he was leaving her for Europe directly, but her witch's intuition told her there would be another act in the drama" (Guest 26). Her intuition was very accurate, for Pound's departures and reappearance's would become a recurring theme in H.D.'s life; although often tumultuous, their relationship was nevertheless, lifelong.

Accompanying her fears of losing Pound were deeper fears of losing Frances Gregg, the young actress and writer who had become H.D.'s closest companion during Ezra's frequent absences. Entering into a deep and romantic friendship with Gregg, H.D. forever alluded to her as the love of her life. Strangely, while Frances had been H.D.'s inseparable companion, the poet became distressed to find that while she was worrying over what to do with Pound, Frances had formed a romantic attachment to him, as well. "Two girls in love with each other, and each in love with the same man," wrote Gregg in her journal, "Frances, Hilda, Ezra." However, the romance between Gregg and Pound did not develop, and H.D. seemed reconciled to them both.

Knowing that Pound was leaving shortly for Europe to begin his attempt at world stardom in earnest, H.D. contemplated a trip abroad herself. When Gregg and her mother announced their intention of taking a European vacation, H.D. went with them. Although Guest suggests that H.D.'s initial trip to Europe was to join Pound, there were other factors behind her desire to leave home. Since her failure at college, H.D. had occupied her time reading, writing, assisting her mother, and visiting; at twenty-five, she was tired of playing the role of dutiful daughter (and little more) in Upper Darby, Pennsylvania. Put plainly, she was bored, unchallenged, lonely, and keenly aware that the role of wife and mother would never be enough to satisfy her.

Even as she wished to join Pound, H.D. was aware that, while bound emotionally and artistically, their relationship was draining and romantically impermanent. In *Paint it Today*, she describes her engagement to Pound as but "the shadow of an understanding" (22). Recounting in her first novel the confusion and sense of ennui that plagued her in 1911, H.D. writes,

> [s]he was desperate and tired and weary in her very early twenties. What chemistry and the binomial theorem had not drained from her of avidity and living fervor, the male adolescent had. She had not the strength nor courage to snap fresh and vivid from the surroundings of her childhood. She had no sap or vivid living power left in her. She felt instinctively that she was a failure by all the conventional and scholarly standards. She had failed her college career, she had failed as a social asset with her family and the indiscriminate mob of relatives and relays of communal friends that surrounded it. She had burned her candle of rebellion at both ends and she was left unequipped for the simplest dealings in the world. (*Paint it Today* 7)

From her own account, H.D. seemed prepared to go anywhere which might ease her sense of failure and unhappiness. Although she loved her family and her home, H.D. was ill at ease there, in part because of her ambiguous relationship with Pound, her increasing awareness of her two sexualities, and her mother's insistent interference. Perhaps even more important was her growing need to be surrounded by writing and writers. The company of her mother, the annoying presence of her sister-in-law, and the occasional companionship of her father and brothers could not satisfy

H.D.'s craving for "people of letters," nor could it assuage her general sense of ennui.

Friedman cites H.D.'s need to go abroad after Pound's departure, suggesting the depth of H.D.'s desire for intellectual and artistic stimulation as consistently great. Moreover, Friedman maintains that H.D.'s "intellectual and artistic awakenings had their source in personal interactions" (1). H.D.'s *Notes on Thought and Vision* echoes these sentiments:

> All reasoning, normal, sane and balanced men and women need and seek at certain times of their lives, certain definite physical relationships. Men and women of temperament, musicians, scientists, artists especially, need these relationships to develop and draw forth their talents. Not to desire and make every effort to develop along these natural physical lines, cripples and dwarfs the being. To shun, deny and belittle such experiences is to bury one's talent carefully in a napkin. (17)

H.D.'s phrasing here is notable, both for its ambiguous articulation of what types of physical relationships she means (her use of the word "definite" does little to clarify), and also for its iteration of her need and desire for these relationships. In the passage, the frequently reclusive and reticent H.D. admits that it is her "physical" contact with others which stimulates both her and her art. Here, as in the *Sea Garden* poems, H.D. alludes to the link between sexuality and artistic fulfillment, indeed, to its role as the genesis of creativity itself. While sexual relationships would play a great role in H.D.'s life as both woman and artist, she also felt a deep need for companionship. She needed the physical presence of other creative individuals around her. Notably, it is Pound's role as companion, mentor, and intellectual "sparring partner" that made him such a lasting part of her life, not the brief part he played as "fiance." Without outside stimulation, H.D.'s creativity could potentially have remained dormant. Once Pound was gone, contact with the artistic and intellectual community H.D. so admired was greatly reduced; for the sake of her creativity and intellect, if the community would no longer come to her by way of Pound, she would have to go to it.

H.D.'s initial response to Paris was lukewarm. Arriving in Europe in 1911 accompanied by Frances and Mrs. Gregg, H.D. found that the city was not pleasant; the Louvre was closed, and the accommodations were small. Soon, these minor inconveniences would cease to bother H.D. as she began to appreciate the historicity, the "age" of Europe. Disembarking with Frances Gregg at Etaples, H.D. described their boat as

> an Andros, or Arcadia or Helenis stranded there from southern waters. They had really not touched the south here. Yet they saw in the sifted evening light that caught the surface of a sea pool far up on the flat beach a suggestion of some holy inland lake. At least, it was Josepha who said it made her think of a scene from Galilee. (*Paint it Today* 15)

Entranced by artifacts and individuals representing hundreds of years of history, H.D. was awed by Europe; the sense of age, of times past and indeed, the passage of time itself pervades H.D.'s accounts of her first experiences in Europe. Her increasingly passionate relationship with Frances Gregg romanticizes and further complicates these accounts; both *Paint it Today* and *Asphodel* are curious blends of personal, cultural, and historical contemplation. Embedded in these contemplations are H.D.'s struggles to define her national identity (as an American abroad) and her sexuality (her relationships with Pound and Gregg).

These struggles with self-definition are evident in the first few pages of *Asphodel* when Hermione [H.D.], Clara, and Fayne [Frances] are mistaken as Englishwomen by a group of children who cry, "Engl-ees. Engl-eesh. Beef-steak" (6). While H.D.'s text notes their error, it also begs the question of how American Hermione and Fayne really are. "O Clara they think we're Engl-eesh" remarks Hermione (*Asphodel* 6), using the same French pronunciation of the word English used by the children. Indeed, Hermione goes on to address the children and several other people in a dialogue of broken English for several paragraphs which terminate with the cryptic, "O France let me die here, let me die, press me to you, beautiful book, a flower's leaf floated here by chance, a moth with dried wings spread out . . . between your vivid pages" (7).

Paint it Today similarly questions H.D.'s national identity as she discusses "the Americans" or "transplanted Europeans" as if removed from them, assuring herself of her own cultural adaptability. She fits in with European society so well, her "Americanness" comes as a surprise. "They looked at Midget [H.D.], tall to the break-in-the-middle point, with fluttering hat brim and tenuous ankles, as of their own world, too young to be noticed or to be regarded suddenly with a jerk in the midst of pleasant, normal conversation, suddenly on guard as if, unwittingly, they had betrayed themselves. 'What *you*, an American?'" (*Paint it Today* 18-19). Even as H.D. declares her nationality, saying "yes, she was an American" (*Paint it Today* 19), the insistence on naming her "true" identity is wasted, both for the ambiguity caused by the past tense ("was") and by H.D.'s subsequent remark that "[l]anguage and tradition do not make a people" (*Paint it Today* 20). Although it seems as if H.D. claims her American identity, the continual questioning of nationality leaves this aspect of her identity ambiguous and indeterminate.

By the time she reached England, H.D.'s vision of Europe had lost any remnants of negativity; transformed from a rather unpleasant place, Europe became "home" as the young poet realized she had no desire to return to America. Introduced into the society of British poets, artists, and musicians, H.D. "found the creative stimulation and support she required to begin her artistic career in the avant-garde milieu of London" (Friedman 2). Statuesque, artistic, unusual, the elegant and distant H.D. was, in

England at least, quite a success. Gregg, however, was not. Guest describes Frances as "too impetuous and forthright for the British. Despite her secretly sworn love for Frances, she [H.D.] was relieved when the Greggs decided to return home. Hilda would be on her own, and with the help of Ezra, heaven knew what she might accomplish" (28).

As Friedman notes, H.D. recognized Gregg's unsuitability for European society, describing her as middle-class and suspicious. "Josepha [Gregg], through prenatal accident and the shocks attending a precarious childhood, had learned early to distrust them. She was, in turn, more or less avoided by them. Her eyes discountenanced them" (*Paint it Today* 18). The "prenatal accident" to which H.D. refers implies that Josepha (Frances) has a "natural" distrust of foreigners or the typical zenophobia experienced by Americans abroad. On a deeper level, however, this could also be a veiled reference to H.D.'s description of Josepha as a "natural" invert or what Ellis describes as a "congenital invert" (*Studies in the Psychology of Sex* 1:4 14). If we were to agree with this possibility, it would seem to exemplify H.D.'s tendency to exercise a sort of "sexual suitability." While in America, H.D. had needed Frances Gregg in Pound's absence and therefore had responded to her as a lesbian; here on the shores of Europe with a new and exciting social set, H.D. perhaps wished to distance herself from Frances in an attempt at exercising her heterosexual self. This would seem plausible for during her early years in Europe, H.D.'s romantic liaisons were predominantly heterosexual. Although this sounds callous, torn between her desire to be a social and artistic success in London and her desire for Frances, H.D.'s feelings could not have been so simple and for a time, H.D.'s initial relief at the departure of Gregg and her mother turned quickly into regret.

With Pound's engagement to another woman ensuring a complete break of their romantic bond, H.D. would be left nearly alone. Moreover, the relationship with Frances was far deeper than that she had shared with Pound. Frances had been H.D.'s "light" in a frequently dark and lonely existence (*Paint it Today* 7); their love affair had opened up a new world for H.D. Appreciating the impact of Frances Gregg on H.D. is crucial to an understanding of her life and work. As H.D. herself explains, "[t]he worlds had broken down, all the worlds, at least all the reasonable and reasoning worlds filled with all the people of reason, parents, every friend, the shadow of the erstwhile fiancé, who had guessed at something but who had never penetrated beyond the worlds of today" (*Paint it Today* 10). While their sexual relationship may have terminated, H.D. would persistently return to Frances Gregg in her work, referring to her as a sort of touchstone, representing a love that could never be extinguished.

Upon Frances' return to the United States, H.D. took an increasingly active role in London "society." Introduced by the successful and commanding Pound, H.D.'s acceptance was assured. Writing to Pound's mother, Isabel, H.D. explained, "Ezra has been so good to me introducing me to celebrities and lesser oddities-he always has some underdog on hand." Even after the termination of her romance with Pound and the loss of Gregg, H.D. viewed her transatlantic crossing as the beginning of a new life and a new identity. Where formerly her height, introspection, and dramatic posturing had forced H.D. to the margins of American society, in England, these characteristics were celebrated. Even her indeterminate sexuality did not work against her in London's art world.

For the senior Doolittles, however, H.D.'s stay in Europe was upsetting. H.D.'s mother and father had no desire for her to remain alone in European society, and her stubborn refusal to come home was difficult to tolerate. The matter was settled when H.D.'s parents joined her in Europe; after much argument, they eventually allowed her to stay. Only after her parents departure did H.D. completely transform from an academically unsuccessful and gauche young American to "H.D., Imagiste"; as she describes in *Paint it Today*, until her refusal to return home, H.D.'s life had been controlled by her parents. At age twenty-five she was ready to stand her ground:

> I should have rebelled long ago. It is not that I am callous. I have really, and that has been the trouble from the first, been far too tender-hearted. I have not been half rebellious enough. If I had begun at fifteen instead of now, things would have been all right. I should never, never have submitted to geometry. (40)

In the novel, Mrs. Defreddie [H.D.'s mother], wants to know why her daughter will not return home to America. Midget [H.D.] explodes in response. Replying both to the question and to the years of blasé existence in Pennsylvania in the staid and repressive household of her mother, Midget imagines a tirade which includes an imaginary matricide:

> Your mother, your mother, your mother, the present said to Midget, has betrayed or would betray, through the clutch and the tyranny of the emotion, your father, the mind in you, the jewel the king, your father gave you as your birthright. Look, said the present, and choose. Here is a knife, slay your mother. She has betrayed or would betray that gift. (*Paint it Today* 43)

The desire to kill her mother denotes H.D.'s resistance to returning to America; she would rather commit murder than return. Moreover, it illustrates H.D.'s ambiguous sexual feelings regarding her mother and father and does so in an acutely Freudian fashion. From a psychoanalytic viewpoint, the "imaginary" execution of her mother and "object selection" of her father represent H.D.'s individual progression toward sexual maturity. Further, as the passage indicates, H.D. quickly moves beyond this attraction/rejection of her parents in favor of her own independence. This movement illustrates the writer's progression beyond her initial "incestuous phantasies" to a higher level of maturity by "breaking away from . . .

parental authority" altogether (*Contributions to the Theory of Sex* 617-18). However, the movement toward independence did not prevent H.D. from revisiting her relationship with her mother repeatedly, both through her prose, and her relationships with other women.

Perhaps more important than the Freudian implications of the passage is H.D.'s acknowledgment that her father is responsible for her gift. "That gift" (*Paint it Today* 43) was H.D.'s intellect and creative ability as a writer; always boastful of her father's scientific mind, H.D. would often refer to her intellectual and creative capacity as a sort of genetic hand-me-down from him. Aware of Darwin's statements regarding inherited traits and their relationship to the further evolution of intellectual development, H.D. perhaps questioned whether her high intellect, and her creative drive, were examples of evolutionary progression, particularly as they manifested themselves through the manipulation of language. Darwin denotes man's acquisition of language as an important evolutionary marker, arguing that

> [a] great stride in the development of the intellect will have followed, as soon as the half-art and half-instinct of language came into use; for the continued use of language will have reacted on the brain and produced an inherited effect; and this again will have reacted in the improvement of language. (*The Descent of Man* 912)

Viewing herself as the product of her grandfather and father, both author-scientists, H.D. perhaps made a connection between her genetic ties to her literary forebears, her own experimentation with language, and the progressive "improvement of language" referred to by Darwin.

Although she had been sensitive to her mother's desire for her to be a "normal" woman, to learn the arts of domesticity, to marry and have children, H.D. was now torn. Which was her more natural path? Was it her duty to be a "normal" woman like her mother or to be a writer like her father and grandfather? While she understood duty to be exemplified by her mother's position as wife and mother, keeper of hearth and home, H.D. also believed that it was her duty to fulfill her potential, to utilize her "gift." To cast it aside in order to fulfill her gendered position as woman in the sense that her mother had would be to carry out one duty while ignoring another. H.D. would wage a battle between these two roles of author and mother her entire life.

Knowing the disparity between H.D.'s desires and her mother's desires for her polarized the author's feelings about her parents, her writing, and her identity. Taking this into account, H.D.'s choice to metaphorically kill her mother in order to become a writer seems understandable. By "killing" her mother, H.D. terminates the dutiful relationship associated with the love and relative comfort of home in order to pursue her writing career and her personal independence. It prohibits a return to the family which would be fatal to her creative ability; even as she loved Mrs. Doolittle, H.D. recognized that her mother, talented pianist and artist, "lost her gift by allowing her father to frighten her into the role of dutiful daughter," a situation H.D. would not allow her mother or father to replicate with her (Morris, *Signets* 73). The matricide also potentially ends H.D.'s lifetime of indeterminacy caused by her sense of incompleteness when away from her mother, as mentioned in Chapter One. However, the potential for this and its actual occurrence are chasms apart. While H.D. may have attempted to terminate the bonds which confined her to her mother and end the extended period of arrested development these bonds caused, her attempt was not, ultimately, successful, as is clear by the continued presence of the mother figure in both her figure and her poetry. Indeed, the Helen myth gets seemingly greater as H.D. matures.

Realizing at last that "the gift" her father has passed on to her was ready to find an outlet in London's society of artists, although fearful of a complete breach with her tight-knit family, H.D. would not be daunted. As she explains, "[i]f she went away [from home and family], her spirit would break, if she stayed, she would be suffocated" (HERmione 9). Strangely, even while H.D. was determined not to replicate her mother's stifled existence, her own role as mother would play an important part in the creation of future works. H.D.'s complicated feelings towards her mother would become intertwined with her own feelings about what motherhood meant; her confused and ambiguous identity in the mother/child relationship with her mother was symptomatic of a similarly complex mother/child relationship with her daughter, and with her work. Later in life, H.D. would claim the womb as the nexus of feminine power and creativity; evidence of this is her writing of the "womb-brain" or "over-mind" and her belief that both human and textual "children" are products of the womb's creative power: "Should we be able to think with the womb and feel with the brain? . . . The brain and the womb are both centres of consciousness, equally important" (*Notes on Thought and Vision* 20-21).

Donna Hollenberg emphasizes the complexity of H.D.'s feelings regarding mother/child relations and their importance to the writer's creativity, extending her discussion to incorporate the multiple difficulties underlying feminine creativity; forced to confront issues regarding her own mother as both parent and female role model, as well as to examine the positive and negative elements of the mother/child bond, the writer's role as creator is further complicated by her tenuous position as woman/author/mother in a society dominated by males. Hollenberg explains,

> [s]ince a woman reexperiences herself as a cared-for child when she becomes a mother, her identification with her own mother often revives issues from her childhood that have remained unresolved. H.D.'s trauma in pregnancy bound up this identification and increased her anxiety about the mother's role in a male-dominated society. Thus the reconciliation of motherly virtue with intellectual achievement, unavailable to most women when H.D. was a child, became of paramount importance to her identity as a women writer. (33)

As Hollenberg points out, most modern women did not have mothers who engaged in intellectual pursuits; they therefore were forced to negotiate the realms of their creativity as untrodden terrain. In H.D.'s case, her mother gave up her role as artistic creator to please both her father and husband; knowing this, the writer felt an internal resistance to "being like her mother" while simultaneously wishing to replicate her mother's "motherliness." When the anxiety caused by her position as both mother and child is examined alongside her genetic predisposition to "be like her father," as well as her growing awareness of her two sexual identities, H.D.'s reliance on contemporary sex theories as explications of human behavior seems not only understandable, but logical.

Because her mother had rejected the creative aspect of her identity which is so tied to sexuality and motherhood, she could not provide H.D. with explanations for her own sexual, creative, or motherly identity; moreover, because these rejections occurred at Mr. Doolittle's behest, H.D. was confused. Even as her father had bestowed on her a creative gift, he had simultaneously demanded that her mother reject her own creativity. Receiving no clear examples from either parent, H.D. therefore created her own explanations of who and what she was through a translation and transformation of the theories of the sexologists. The result would be two distinctly separate or "twin" selves, rather than one unified whole; the polarity of these two selves is evidenced in her relationships with men and women and in her two major artistic forms.

It seems likely that Havelock Ellis had the most direct influence on H.D.'s early prose works, for his theories regarding inversion and female creativity are very evocative of her position as female author and intellectual. Reading Ellis's remarks that "in literature, homosexuality in women has furnished a much more frequent motive to the artist than homosexuality in men" (*Studies in the Psychology of Sex* 1:4 198), H.D. could hardly have failed to associate herself with these ideas; *Paint it Today*, *HERmione*, and *Asphodel* all have an intense lesbian relationship as their thematic center. Interestingly, Ellis also notes that it is "among the upper ranks, alike of society and of prostitution, that Lesbianism is most definitely to be met with, for here we have much greater liberty of action, and much greater freedom from prejudices" (*Studies in the Psychology of Sex* 1:4 216), an idea reminiscent of Shari Benstock's discussion of lesbian expatriates in modern Paris.

In *Women of the Left Bank*, Benstock notes that "the expatriate female Modernist" was "a woman whose intellectual and sexual independence was secured by financial privilege and social distinction" (9). Benstock explains that while not all expatriate female Modernists were extremely wealthy, like Nancy Cunard or Winifred Ellerman (Bryher), most of them were comfortably middle class, Gertrude Stein and Alice Toklas, for example. Benstock further notes that the expatriate female moderns "all received similar educations-studying music, painting, or literature" (*Women of the*

Left Bank 10), supportive evidence of Ellis's theory that educated women are more likely to engage in open lesbianism. Although Benstock claims that Natalie Barney, perhaps the most famous of the lesbian moderns, adamantly opposed Ellis's theory of inversion for its link to degeneracy, many of the moderns overlooked this aspect of Ellis and focused on his analysis that many inverts were intellectually gifted. H.D. was among them.

Even as she negotiated her ambiguous sexuality and nationality in 1911-12, one aspect of H.D.'s identity was becoming increasingly clear: her identity as a writer. To be a writer had been what she desired; it had only taken the courage to break free, courage which had been inspired by the success of Pound, the loss of Gregg, and H.D.'s acceptance by the British. The creation of H.D. as writer therefore directly coincided with the recreation of H.D. as expatriated American; although she had made attempts at writing prior to her expatriation, it was after being accepted into London society, patronized by novelist and social benefactor May Sinclair, and protégée of Pound, that H.D. began to consider her writing as truly important. The warm reception of London's society left H.D. with a strong allegiance to her new home. While not changing her citizenship, this allegiance certainly affected her national sympathies. By the end of 1911, H.D. had become an Anglophile; appreciative of her height, her elegant beauty, her desire for knowledge and creative inspiration, England's artsy set had embraced H.D. wholeheartedly. Unable to forget her awkward and lonely social position back home, H.D. willingly undertook expatriation. Tellingly, she would marry British poet Richard Aldington hastily, both as a response to Pound's rejection and as evidence of her desire to "become" European. With her marriage, H.D. officially gained British citizenship, allowing her to stay in England indefinitely.

Bid Me to Live chronicles H.D.'s marriage, her increasing British sympathy, and her horror of war. In the book, H.D. clearly distinguishes between herself and "the Americans," and unlike *Paint it Today* and *Asphodel*, she does not undercut this distinction by claiming her American nationality. With her marriage to Aldington, H.D. decisively renounces her American identity, and nationality ceases to be ambiguous. Her denouncement of American citizenship would last for more than forty years. Not until 1958, after many years of living in England and Switzerland, would H.D. regain her American citizenship through an oath of allegiance. Here again we see evidence that rather than a duality, nationality for H.D. was *one or the other*, dependant upon the emotions ascendant at the time.

Moreover, while her marriage to Richard Aldington ended her sense of having two nationalities, it likewise temporarily arrested H.D.'s two sexualities or more accurately, her sexual polarity, for unlike the novels preceding it, in *Bid Me To Live*, the H.D. character, Julia, is strictly heterosexual.

Swimming Upstream

> Love is profoundly animal; therein is its beauty.
> —Remy de Gourmont

Much speculated on, H.D.'s marriage to Aldington is discussed by critics and biographers rather dubiously; Robinson declares it to be a "rebellious marriage," directly relating it to Pound's engagement to Dorothy Shakespear. However, the biographer complicates the issue by stating that "[i]n her imaginative life, H.D. associated Aldington first with the city of Paris and later with the mythological Paris who had stolen Helen from Menelaus" (Robinson 42). Her identity clearly in flux, Robinson implies that H.D. wished to attach herself concretely to the continent representative of her acceptance as an artist and intellectual; nothing could link her more directly to her new country than marriage. Louis Silverstein likewise notes the connection between H.D.'s relationship with Aldington and her "love affair" with Europe, stating that H.D. would "associate her love for Aldington with their travels and courtship in Italy, especially Rome" (*Signets* 34). However, Robinson suggests that even as H.D. was transforming herself into a European, she still kept much of her "waspish" American morality intact; by marrying a British poet, H.D. could somehow finally fulfill her desire for creativity and the arts while simultaneously fulfilling her duty as woman and Moravian. Robinson explains:

> Her upbringing had, of course, taught her to have no romantic involvement that would not lead to marriage. For years she had been involved in the idealistic notion of a poetic relationship modeled on the marriage of Robert and Elizabeth Browning. In fact, the Brownings, whom she had learned about from Pound, were a major influence on H.D. as models for future literature and life. (42)

H.D. may have harbored some romantic notions about replicating the relationship of the Victorian Brownings; however, the reality of her 1913 marriage to Aldington was a far cry from the dream. With *Bid Me to Live*, H.D. describes the relationship with Aldington harshly, stating that "[t]hey might have made a signal success of their experiment. They made a signal success of it, but in the tradition not so much of Robert Browning and Elizabeth Barrett as of Punch and Judy" (11). The tragicomic view of her marriage is not overstated; although initially physically attracted to Aldington, H.D.'s relationship with him was frequently tumultuous and abusive. Gregarious, handsome, and often charming, Aldington was not cerebral enough to suit H.D. His sometimes disappointing intellect, combined with his rather brutish sexuality and occasional crudity, made Aldington appear mediocre and somewhat offensive when compared to the sharp-tongued, aesthetically high-minded, and witty Pound. Aldington's lack of emotional depth also made him a poor replacement for Frances Gregg. Shortly after the stillbirth of her first child in 1915, which caused her great emotional pain for years afterward, H.D. realized that her two-year marriage was in distress; while the Aldingtons remained together "officially" until their separation in 1919 when H.D. began her relationship with Bryher (Winifred Ellerman), Aldington's time away in the service, combined with his numerous extramarital affairs, doomed the relationship long before H.D.'s departure. Strangely, while H.D. and Aldington separated in 1919, they did not divorce until 1938.

The years between her initial transatlantic crossing of 1911 and the oath of allegiance reaffirming her American citizenship in 1958 were years of creative, sexual, and national experimentation and transformation for H.D. After her break with Aldington, she gave birth to daughter Perdita, struggled with her writing, and traveled extensively with Bryher. During one of their many excursions, H.D. and Bryher spent time in Paris where they were occasional guests at the home of Gertrude Stein; at Stein's salon, H.D. met numerous women writers whom Benstock refers to as "the Expatriate Sapphic Modernists." Where Pound had been H.D.'s creative inspiration during her early years as an Imagist, the presence of these other female moderns was just as influential on her later work in both prose and extended poems. The Sapphic moderns revised H.D.'s self-perception as both woman and poet; the creative experimentation of their work acted as a catalyst for her own exploratory prose, and the open lesbianism and bisexuality of Natalie Barney, Djuna Barnes, Stein and others helped H.D. to realize that her ambiguous, fluctuating sexuality was not unique among the moderns. As Benstock notes, "Sapphic modernism wore many stylistic faces . . . wore many necessary and elaborate disguises, making it almost impossible for the literary historian to categorize and group its various occurrences" (185). Reading both the sexually coded and overtly lesbian texts of the Sapphic moderns, H.D. wrote numerous exploratory works, both prose and poetry. Indeed, it was perhaps during her stay in Paris that H.D. realized that her attraction toward both men and women was as important to her creativity as was motherhood.

While the Sapphic moderns were an important influence on H.D., Pound and Aldington's earlier reading and translating of Remy de Gourmont's *The Natural Philosophy of Love* also appears to have impacted her. Gourmont's work was an evolutionary treatise, of sorts, differing from Darwin primarily in its more graphic account of the sex act itself. Further, while Darwin acknowledged that man was a species, he implied that as a species, man was, to date, the most highly "evolved." De Gourmont disagreed, viewing man as just another animal. "On reflection," stated De Gourmont, "one will consider the different love-mechanisms of all the dioicians as parallel and contemporary. Man will then find himself in his proper and rather indistinct place in the crowd, beside the monkeys, rodents, and bats" (*The Natural Philosophy of Love* 6).

De Gourmont's narrative is sexually explicit and focuses more specifically on the physical manifestations of human love than does Darwin's. It is perhaps this sexual explicitness that appealed to H.D.; while her upbringing reinforced heterosexuality and feminine modesty, thus discouraging her from acting on her sexual impulses, De Gourmont's frankness and negation of sexual denial must have been refreshing if not always accurate.

After moving to Europe and writing poetry extensively, H.D. took up her prose writing in earnest as she began to chronicle the important relationships of her life; the emotional and intellectual ties which bound her to both Pound and Gregg typify a sexual ambiguity and complexity which would be manifested repeatedly in H.D.'s life and work. This sexually ambiguous aspect of her identity is particularly arresting in its seemingly unselfconscious presence in H.D.'s prose works. Her simultaneous love affairs with Pound and Gregg are examined together in *Paint it Today*, and although H.D. implies in the novel that the deeper bond is forged with Gregg, she nevertheless insists on the validity of her relationship with Pound. While much of the freedom to express her attractions to men and women arose in response to H.D.'s reading of and interacting with the Sapphic moderns, I argue that just as important to this relative freedom was her reading of Havelock Ellis and Sigmund Freud. As noted above, Ellis correlated high intellect and creative genius with sexual inversion, and although his tendency to associate degeneration with inversion was problematic for H.D., she would surely have been appreciative of the link he made between creativity and sexual inversion or hermaphroditism. As with her treatment of Freud, H.D. would apparently take what she wished from Ellis and disregard that which simply did not apply to her.

Like Ellis, Freud also links high intellect with sexual inversion; unlike Ellis, however, Freud negates the degenerative aspect of inversion by first qualifying the definition of degeneration and then discounting its applicability to inversion. This qualification is worth noting in full:

> It has, in fact, become customary to designate all morbid manifestations not of traumatic or infectious origin as degenerative. Indeed, Magnan's classification of degenerates makes it possible to apply the concept of degeneration to the most general forms of nervous activity. Under such circumstances, it may be asked whether the idea of "degeneration" is still of any use, or whether it has new meaning. It would seem more appropriate not to speak of degeneration: (1) where there are not many marked deviations from the normal; (2) where the capacity for working and living do not in general appear markedly impaired.

That inverts are not degenerates in this qualified sense can be seen from the following facts:

> The inversion is found in people who otherwise show no marked deviation from the normal.

> It is found also in people whose mental capacities are not disturbed, who on the contrary are distinguished by especially high intellectual development and ethical culture.
> If one disregards the patients of one's own practice and strives to comprehend a wider field of experience, he will encounter facts in two directions, which will prevent him from considering inversion as a sign of degeneration. (*Contributions to the Theory of Sex* 555-6)

Freud's discounting of inversion as degeneration and subsequent recategorization of inversion as a "perversion" was a groundbreaking approach to homosexuality. Moving beyond his incomplete and "male-oriented" theory of the masculinity complex as responsible for lesbianism, Freud's articulation of "sexuality as perversion" is far more comprehensive in its applicability to lesbians, including "feminine" lesbians who had "baffled sexologists and psychoanalysts" (*The Practice of Love* xiii). De Lauretis suggests that,

> if perversion is understood with Freud outside the moralistic, religious, or medical frames of reference, as a deviation of the sexual drive from the path leading to the reproductive object-that is to say, if homosexuality is merely another path taken by the drive in its cathexis or choice of object, rather than a pathology (although, like every other aspect of sexuality, it may involve pathogenic elements)-then Freud's theory contains or implies, if by negation and ambiguity, a notion of perverse desire, where perverse simply means not pathological but rather non-heterosexual or non-normatively heterosexual. (xiii)

While Ellis was an important early influence on H.D. and her writing, as a "womanly woman," she no doubt found Freud's theories regarding female sexuality as a perversion much more applicable to her life and identity. Seeking answers both for her creative and sexual self, intrigued by Freud's discussions of perversion, fixation, desire, and repression, H.D. underwent psychoanalysis with several analysts in the hopes of understanding her shifting sexuality and its relationship to her work; in 1933-34, she was treated by Freud himself.

As we examine H.D.'s fluctuations from lesbian to heterosexual to lesbian and often back again, we can perceive these sexual shifts as keys to understanding the numerous genres H.D. experimented with throughout her career. She was an explorer, both sexually and artistically, continually maintaining a space on a creative and sexual spectrum reminiscent of Adrienne Rich's lesbian continuum. Seldom in her life did H.D. declare herself as consistently one or the other in any aspect of her life; instead, she far more consistently described herself as something in between or at either end. Lidia Yukman notes this "in betweenness" as integral to understanding H.D.'s importance as a modern author, suggesting that

> [f]ew writers have managed to hold open the interval between "opposite" the way H.D. did. Her poetry and prose relentlessly mark the borderline between subject and object, between dreamscape and logic, between categories of sexual difference. Her work falls within a historical moment between 1900 and 1950 in which psychosexual explorations surged, particularly in the work of Sigmund Freud and Havelock Ellis. While H.D.'s novels exhibit formal experimentations consistent with modernism, it is her sexual and textual politics that make her unique among modernist writers. (124)

Just as her shifting sexuality was integral to H.D.'s creativity, as I will discuss further in Chapter Seven, so, too, was her national identity; it would shift from American to European and back again. This national identity, like her sexuality, would be heavily influenced by those around her, fluctuating in response to her intimate romantic and artistic relationships. These fluctuations in identity are most evident in the prose works chronicling each significant relationship in her life. Commenting on H.D.'s non-linear and recursive style, Yukman identifies the prose texts as products of a specific bisexual linguistic strategy, "emphasizing an identity in process through a specifically syntactic refusal to commit to binary oppositions" (*Representing Bisexualities: Subject and Cultures of Fluid Desire* 125). Yukman seems accurate in her insistence on H.D.'s "refusal to commit to binary oppositions": commitment to one or the other was impossible. Instead, sexually, nationally, and creatively, H.D.'s narrative and identity have as their only constant the notion of change and transformativity. This constant transformative process was one she shared with another modern, Ernest Hemingway.

CHAPTER FIVE

Distant Observations

> So you fought, he thought. And in the fighting soon there was no purity of feeling for those who survived the fighting and were good at it. Not after the first six months.
> —Ernest Hemingway

Hemingway's first journey to Europe as a soldier in 1918 was a life-changing experience he recreated repeatedly in both his short works and his novels. Going off to war out of both a sense of adventure and patriotic duty, the youthful Hemingway must have imagined himself a hero, much like his grandfathers, both of whom were decorated veterans of the Civil War; however, after seeing combat with the Ambulance Corps, Hemingway's youthful enthusiasm for war rapidly diminished. Death and disposal of the dying was not the sport he had fancifully imagined. Wounded at Fossalta by an Austrian Minenwerfer, Hemingway's naïve and heroic view of combat was completely erased.

Scott Donaldson claims that after the wounding, "Ernest feared that if he ever shut his eyes in the dark and let himself go, his soul would fly out of his body like a handkerchief" (*By Force of Will* 126). Hemingway mentions the fear of the dark which accompanied his wounding in "A Way You'll Never Be" when Nick Adams tells Paravicini, "I'm all right. I can't sleep without a light of some sort. That's all I have now" (*The Complete Short Stories* 309). Moreover, although "[h]is injury at Fossalta hardly provided the only key to unlock his writing and his personality," while in Europe during WWI Hemingway certainly "did abandon there his romantic concept of combat, to be replaced by a healthy disillusionment about war in general and World War I in particular" (Donaldson 126).

"A Way You'll Never Be" is a fierce and ironic depiction of the disillusionment Donaldson mentions, as protagonist Nick Adams is sent back to the Italian front to model the American uniform in the hopes of raising morale. Nick and Paravicini both know that no other Americans will be coming to the aid of the wretchedly small and doomed battalion, and while both try to behave civilly, Nick's attempt at optimism fails. After riding past a recent massacre, his shell-shocked psyche submits to delusions; repeatedly trying to get a grip on himself in order to be of some small service to this group of Italians he knows are soon to die, Nick finally gets on his bicycle and rides off. The story is chilling in its realistic understatement and damning in its accusations regarding America's ineffectual involvement in the war. When the adjutant asks Nick if the Italians will soon be receiving American assistance, Nick replies sarcastically,

> Oh, absolutely. Americans twice as large as myself, healthy, with clean hearts, sleep at night, never been wounded, never been blown up, never had their heads caved in, never been scared, don't drink, faithful to the girls they left behind them, many of them never had crabs, wonderful chaps. You'll see. (*The Complete Short Stories* 311)

His description of the Americans who will come is, ironically, evocative of the prewar Nick himself. Nick has been so damaged by the war, one of the Italians has to ask him if in fact he actually is American, and if so, is he from North or South America? This is so reminiscent of the French children who are amazed at H.D.'s "Americanness" that it gives one pause. Strangely, not unlike H.D., Hemingway's American identity, like his patriotism, has been nearly erased due to the loss of his youth, his health, and his idealism.

The questioning of nationality arises again in several Hemingway "war" stories, including the novel, *A Farewell to Arms*. A more developed characterization of Hemingway's transformation from youthful idealist to cynical realist, Frederic Henry, the protagonist in *A Farewell to Arms*, initially enlists in the Italian army because he thinks "the cause is just," but quickly realizes that it is instead, "all a sham" (Donaldson 128). Like his creator, Frederic Henry loses his sense of duty and nationalism, taking no pride in fighting once the "just cause" appears absurd. Frederic Henry is so disgusted with the war, he no longer sees a cause, but more importantly, no longer sees an end. "Still, nobody was whipping any one on the Western front. Perhaps wars weren't won any more. Maybe they went on forever. Maybe it was another Hundred Years' War" (*A Farewell to Arms* 118). For the disillusioned American, "[p]atriotism seems out of place, and indeed most of the patriots whom Frederic meets are at considerable distance from the combat zone" (Donaldson 128).

As Donaldson points out, the only "true" patriot for Frederic Henry after his wounding is the mercenary, Ettore Moretti, who is honest about his reasons for fighting-he's good at it and it pays. He gains something of substance, albeit monetary, from his participation in the war. Donaldson explains Hemingway's mercenary depiction of WWI as illustrative of the author's contempt for what he sees as an exercise in ego and theatricality; the critic suggests that after Hemingway's experiences driving an ambulance, he saw little value in war, one of the most persistent of human undertakings. Hemingway's acknowledgment that the war might go on forever is distinctly evocative of Darwin's articulation of battle as an innate part of nature in the struggle for existence; however, unlike ancient warriors who fought battles "both in the general struggle for life and in their contests for their wives" (*The Descent of Man* 872), the soldiers in WWI are fighting over ideas.

Realizing this, Hemingway must have been struck by the paradox of the great naturalist's concluding remarks in *The Descent of Man* regarding man's moral development as an example of his social instincts. The notions of war and morality initially seem antithetical. Darwin explains:

> These instincts are highly complex, and in the case of the lower animals give special tendencies towards certain definite actions; but the more important elements are love, and the distinct emotion of sympathy. Animals endowed with the social instincts take pleasure in one another's company, warn one another of danger, defend and aid one another in many ways. These instincts do not extend to all the individuals of the species, but only to those of the same community. (*The Descent of Man* 912)

Initially drawn to war out of a desire for adventure, Hemingway had an underlying and sympathetic desire to aid those defending what he had considered to be a highly moral ideal, a motivation indicative of Darwin's remarks above. However, after experiencing the reality that "[t]hese instincts to not extend to all the individuals of the species," Hemingway must have questioned how "highly moral" these instincts were. While one community was fighting desperately, sympathetically, even lovingly for their comrades and country, they were doing so at the expense of the lives of others, and while they may not have been countrymen, they were still men, members of the same species. The futility of war affected Hemingway deeply, and he must have viewed Darwin's statement that "[i]mportant as the struggle for existence has been and even still is, yet as far as the highest part of man's nature is concerned there are other agencies more important" as very ironic (*The Descent of Man* 919), for immediately after WWI, Hemingway saw no evidence of man's higher nature, and his faith in patriotic ideals was nearly lost for some time to come.

The young Hemingway was not merely affected by the futility of war, however, but also by the fact that, war or not, life went on in its usual manner. It was perhaps life's insistent continuity that kept Hemingway from suffering severe mental trauma over what he witnessed in Italy during WWI; even as he dragged the dead and wounded off the battlefield, Hemingway witnessed life going on all around him. Viewing the war almost like a naturalist, Hemingway took note of the incongruity of life continuing in the midst of death in "On the Quai at Smyrna"; in the two-page story, Hemingway's narrator is first struck by the foolishness of a Turkish officer who takes great pains to be offended by a gunner's mate whom he supposes has insulted him. Intervening between the officer and the mate, the narrator comments that, "I told the Turk the man was being sent on board ship and would be most severely dealt with. Oh most rigorously. He felt topping about it. Great friends we were" (*The Complete Short Stories* 63).

The irony of both tone and situation in "On the Quai" continues as the narrator matter-of-factly discusses numerous women who will not give up their dead babies, even after they have been so for six days or more; further, death at the quai is not restricted to the babies, but is also associated with the nameless "nice things floating around" in the water. Disregarding their proximity to the dead human and animal waste, women are giving birth. "You didn't mind the women who were having babies as you did those with the dead ones," states the narrator, "They had them all right. Surprising how few of them died. You just covered them over with something and let them go at it" (*The Complete Short Stories* 64). While Hemingway could not possibly have been as unmoved by what he witnessed during WWI as the narrator appears to be, the author implies that the only way to live through the monstrosity of war is to harden yourself and view the whole scene as a sort of Darwinian landscape depicting the cycle of struggle, death, and birth.

Reconciling himself to the continuity of life even in the face of death was not restricted to scenes of such as those in "On the Quai at Smyrna," however, for upon Hemingway's return to the States, he was forced to deal with the death of the most important romantic relationship of his life thus far. Although Hemingway had been certain that nurse/lover Agnes von Kurowsky would marry him after the war, she instead chose to end their relationship and take up with an Italian lieutenant. Her termination of their relationship shook the youthful Hemingway; while initially crushed and angered by Agnes's behavior, the author would never completely move beyond these initial emotions and allow himself to exercise his great deal of fondness for her.

The complexity of his feelings for Agnes von Kurowsky, including the necessity of his carrying on with his life after her loss, is illustrated in numerous female characters loosely based on her, most particularly, Catherine Barkeley in *A Farewell to Arms*. Although in the novel Frederic Henry loses Catherine to complications arising from childbirth, the death of their love is still a sort of casualty of war, an idea applicable to Hemingway's lost relationship with Agnes to the arms of an Italian.

Death, love and loss constitute much of Hemingway's postwar fiction and these ideas seem coupled with his earlier fears and sexual phobias. For example, while the wounds to Hemingway's legs may have, as biographers insist, resulted in a fear of the dark and an inability to sleep that would persist until the author's death, the wounds could also have subconsciously reinscribed Hemingway's fears of castration. As Freud notes in his discussion of sexual symbols (which he extends as applicable to the subconscious as mentioned earlier), "[t]he genitals may even be represented by other part of the body" (*The Basic Writings* 375). It would follow, then, that when

Hemingway created Jake Barnes in *The Sun Also Rises* he conflated both his fear of castration (Jake's impotence) with his loss of Agnes (the inability to have a romantic relationship with Brett who ultimately favors Romero) to a foreigner.

Both his wounds and his romantic loss potentially resulted in a type of "war neurosis" similar to that experienced by H.D. and could easily be argued as the reason behind the recurring bouts of depression he experienced in later life. These depressive periods, like H.D.'s breakdowns, are evocative of Freud's articulation of war neuroses which he describes as "to be regarded as traumatic neuroses whose occurrence has been made possible or has been promoted by a conflict in the ego" (*Collected Papers* 5:VIII 85). Further, and more importantly as regards H.D. and Hemingway,

> [t]he conflict is between the soldier's old peaceful ego and his new warlike one, and it becomes acute as soon as the peace-ego realized what danger it runs of losing its life owing to the rashness of its newly formed, parasitic double. it would be equally true to say that the old ego is protecting itself from a mortal danger by taking flight into a traumatic neurosis or that it is defending itself against the new ego which it sees is threatening its life. (*Collected Papers* 5:VIII 85)

The split egos which Freud articulates in the passage above accurately describe the prewar and postwar Hemingway. Seemingly, the trauma experienced in war created a new Hemingway; more aggressive and far less idealistic, this older, wiser Hemingway would often appear fractured and broken, as if in conflict with himself. H.D. too would have a split and her wounds experienced in war would also result in a fracturing of the psyche that would periodically result in the bouts of depression that would characterize her breakdowns.

While the neurosis inflicted by war ties the two authors yet again, so does the romanticizing of their first loves. The image of Agnes as "the woman he had always loved" (Lynn 99) is reminiscent of H.D.'s repeated recollection of Frances Gregg. Like Gregg, Agnes von Kurowsky would become less known for her relationship with an author as for her relationship to the characters the author created and recreated in her image.

The loss of Agnes left a great impact on Hemingway; so too, did the return home. Unable to reconcile his post-war identity to his prewar self, Hemingway quarreled bitterly with his mother and felt terribly out of place with the rest of his family. Grace's attempts to interest Hemingway in college met with derision; he ignored any suggestions of education or employment, just as he "ignored her requests that he clean up his unspeakably untidy room" (Lynn 99). What Hemingway failed to realize in 1919 was that simultaneous to his recovery from the war, Grace Hemingway was suffering a breakdown. While Hemingway may have viewed his mother's requests as unsympathetic to his recent trials, he was likewise unable to recognize his mother's own dilemma as she dealt with a seriously debilitating nervous condition.

In their complete self-absorption, mother and son resembled each other more at this time than perhaps at any other in their lives. Sadly, neither could recognize or acknowledge the other's emotional disturbance; even as Grace was writing letters to her husband describing her physical and mental discomfort in an attempt to alleviate them, Hemingway was busy writing stories in order to exorcise similar demons acquired during the war. Many of these stories would deal with actual wartime experiences, as illustrated above; several, however, would deal with a theme close to Hemingway's heart, the struggle to return to civilian life after seeing battle, yet another example of his attempts at reconciling his split egos as defined by Freud theory.

Perhaps the most autobiographical and important of the stories written at this time is "Soldier's Home," in which Hemingway divulges his deep disillusionment, his "unimportant lies" about the war, his family's inability to understand his experience, and his sense of anticlimax and ennui on returning to America. Through Krebs, the story also frankly exposes Hemingway's view of sex as a biological need, rather than a romantic desire. After the sense of sexual urgency caused by the possibility of imminent death in Europe, Hemingway's response to the young and proper girls of his hometown was laissez-faire. The girls seemed gauche and required too much work "to be had." As the narrator explains,

> [h]e would have liked to have a girl but he did not want to have to spend a long time getting her. He did not want to get into the intrigue and the politics. He did not want to have to do any courting. He did not want to tell any more lies. It wasn't worth it. (*The Complete Short Stories* 112-13)

It seems ridiculous to the returning soldier that he must reengage himself in the complications of small town courtship simply to satisfy an urge; as Krebs points out to himself, "[y]ou did not need a girl" (113). Just as ridiculous is the need to ask permission to use the family car; the incongruity of facing an army of enemy soldiers in a battle frequently fought to the death only to return home and have to fight for such things as the family car is too much for Krebs. His situation on returning home mirrors precisely the exasperation Hemingway experienced when he took up residence again in Oak Park. As Lynn notes in Hemingway's biography,

> [w]hat was particularly maddening from Ernest's point of view was that his status hadn't changed after all. It was as if he had never ridden in the backs of ambulances on Saturday nights in Kansas City, or helped to remove the remains of dead women from a field in Lombardy, or felt the pain of shell fragments tearing into his flesh. On the night of his return to Oak Park, Grace had hailed him as a

conquering hero-and the next day had resumed treating him as though he were still a boy. (101)

Matured from the war, he could no longer submit himself to the tight constraints his mother sought to impose; recalling his discomfort with his mother, Hemingway's story, "Soldier's Home" characterizes his disgust with Grace Hemingway's self-perceived martyrdom, particularly at the end of the story when the mother asks Krebs to "kneel and pray with her" (*The Complete Short Stories* 114). Tellingly, Krebs/Hemingway refuses, but feeling sorry for his earlier admittance that he didn't love his mother, the soldier allows his mother to pray for him. The situation with Krebs/Hemingway is precisely that faced by Midget/H.D.: the child's need to break free from parental bonds and seek independence, arguably to finally terminate, albeit unsuccessfully, their mother fixations.

Even while allowing his mother to pray for him, Krebs, like Hemingway, knows that he must move on; no longer bound by his family's religion, his mother's desires, or his father's affection, the character, like the author, must seek his own fate. Although Hemingway put off the complete break with his family long enough to take an extended fishing trip in Michigan, a trip that would serve both as a bridge from his family to living on his own and as the setting for the longest of his short stories, "Big Two Hearted River," after the trip was over, Hemingway moved on. First visiting with family friends, the Dilworths (who would serve as models for the characters in "Up in Michigan"), Hemingway eventually moved on to a small apartment in Petoskey.

In his Petoskey apartment, Hemingway began a lifelong pattern of writing from early morning until midday, a habit he shared with H.D.; much later, Hemingway would attribute this same habit to another writer, the character David Bourne in the posthumously published *The Garden of Eden*. Shortly after taking up residence in Petoskey, Hemingway got a job house-sitting and caring for the teenage son of family friends, Ralph and Harriet Connable. Although the job proved unchallenging, it nevertheless denotes an important time in Hemingway's life as a writer, for during his stay at the Connables', he not only read voraciously (including works by Havelock Ellis), but also wrote profusely. His time at the Connables' produced twenty-six published articles.

1920 was not important simply for Hemingway's stay with the Connables; it was also the year he would realize the depth of his break with family ties, for on his twenty-first birthday, Grace Hemingway presented him with a letter declaring her disappointment and disgust for the son who had so callously "overdrawn" from the bank of his mother's affection. The letter ends with an admonition not to return until Hemingway's "tongue has learned not to insult and shame your mother. When you have changed your ideas and aims in life, you will find your mother waiting to welcome you, whether it be in this world or the next-loving you and longing for your love" (Lynn 118). Rather than succeed in its mission of bringing Hemingway back to the family fold full of apology, Grace's letter instead acted as a catalyst ensuring the writer's independence and efforts for literary success. Like H.D.'s break with her mother, however, Hemingway's would be a break that would haunt him for the rest of his life.

Shortly after the receipt of Grace's epistle, Hemingway moved to Chicago to look for work; in Chicago, he met first wife, Hadley Richardson, whom he would court (contrary to the contempt for courtship illustrated in "Soldier's Home") intently for several months and marry on September 3, 1921. After his marriage to Hadley, Hemingway was more determined than ever to write seriously. Eventually, he and Hadley determined that they could eke out a meager life in Paris, the city where, according to friend Sherwood Anderson, all serious writers were living. Anderson voiced great confidence in Hemingway's abilities; assured of success in Paris, Hemingway and Hadley set off with letters of introduction to numerous expatriated American writers, among them, Gertrude Stein and Ezra Pound.

During the years he spent in Europe, Hemingway would also meet Robert MacAlmon (his first publisher), MacAlmon's wife, Bryher (Winifred Ellerman), and H.D. Although Hemingway makes no reference to Ellerman or H.D. in *A Moveable Feast* as he does to so many of the moderns he knew in Paris, his acquaintance with H.D. is noted in a letter to Gertrude Stein and Alice Toklas (*Ernest Hemingway's Selected Letters: 1917-61* Baker 127). The relationship with H.D. was not a close one, but it is clear that Hemingway's intense friendship with both Ezra Pound and Robert MacAlmon led to some contact with her. Hemingway did, however, develop a relationship with H.D.'s husband Richard Aldington; his appreciation for Aldington's poetry is apparent by the presence of a complete set of Aldington's works in Hemingway's personal library.

Perhaps Hemingway's and H.D.'s polite acquaintance would have been less distant had Hemingway been aware of H.D.'s interest in contemporary sexual theories. As it was, H.D.'s intense shyness prevented a friendship from developing with Hemingway and most of the moderns she encountered; uncomfortable with their tendency towards excess, H.D. preferred to remain aloof. Guest explains that "[f]or the most part the Paris carnival did not interest H.D. She tired of the Dome and the drinking parties. Hemingway gossiped (falsely) to Gertrude Stein that MacAlmon was teaching Bryher to drink. 'Is that in the Greek Tradition?' he asked" (*Herself Defined* 162). Although H.D. did not choose to socialize much with Hemingway during the early 1920s, she did read his work; however, it was not until much later that she appreciated it. As Barbara Guest notes, while H.D. expressed distaste towards "beatniks," by 1960 she had become "fonder of Faulkner and Hemingway" (*Herself Defined* 320).

While Hemingway's initial trip to Europe was instrumental in his maturation, the return to Europe with Hadley, during which he would make numerous contacts with other moderns, was no less important. This return would greatly influence how Hemingway presented his "revised" thoughts on life and war in fictional form; the atmosphere of Paris itself, as well as the artistic connections he made there in 1922, profoundly impacted Hemingway's writing. In Paris, Hemingway would regain some of his lost affection for America; while still struggling with his jaded idealism, Hemingway's time in Paris injected him with a new sense of purpose and artistic direction. Determining that he would write simply and declaratively, disregarding any "ornamentation" (Baker 85), Hemingway embarked on his sojourn in Europe.

Many of his first attempts at writing in Europe resulted in false starts; eventually, however, Hemingway began to write a series of short stories which would "bridge the gap between [his] high school fiction and more ambitious stories" (Baker 60); they would also illustrate Hemingway's lost youth. Influenced heavily by his war-time experiences, these short stories are gritty in their hard-edged commentary on marriage and explicit in their sexuality; "The Three Day Blow" and "Up in Michigan" are but two examples. The intense sexuality of "Up in Michigan" is strong evidence of Hemingway's growing interest in the darker side of human sexual behavior; written shortly after he read Ellis's *The Dance of Life* in 1921 (Baker 77), "Up in Michigan" evokes both a Darwinian and an Ellisian reading.

In the story, youthful charwoman Liz Coates has a romantic fancy for Jim Gilmore, the local blacksmith; noting the black hair on Jim's arms, Liz realizes she likes Jim in a way "that made her feel funny" (*The Complete Short Stories* 59). As the story continues, Liz thinks about Jim nearly constantly, while he seldom appears to think about her at all. Going out of her way to make herself available to Jim, Liz finally gets what she appears to have set out for: a sexual encounter. However, Liz's romantic notions of Jim are nothing like the brutish sexuality he exhibits when they are alone on the dock. Forcing her dress up, Jim imposes himself on the frightened and objecting Liz, and the scene initially reads as a near-rape:

> She was frightened but she wanted it. She had to have it but it frightened her.
> 'You musn't do it, Jim. You musn't.'
> 'I got to. I'm going to. You know we got to.'
> 'No we haven't, Jim. We ain't got to. Oh, it isn't right. Oh, it's so big and it hurts so. You can't. Oh, Jim. Jim. Oh.'
> (*The Complete Short Stories* 62)

Hemingway's sparse narrative is lacking any romantic subterfuge and reveals distinctly Darwinian elements. For example, in *The Descent of Man*, Charles Darwin asserts European [Caucasian] women's sexual attraction to men exhibiting both facial and body hair, that in fact, women are in part responsible for the retention of hair as a secondary sexual characteristic insofar as it is involved in the process of sexual selection (*The Descent of Man* 906).

In the passage above, it is Jim's dark arm hair which distinctly arouses Liz's passion. Further, the lines describing how Liz "wanted it," that she had to have it," echo Darwin's statements regarding humanity's intense biological urge to reproduce as one of two innate desires. The story also illustrates Darwin's theory of sexual selection, for although Liz is passive during the sex scene itself, Hemingway's narrative clearly indicates Liz as the one who selects Jim rather than the reverse.

While Liz's pursuit of a sexual encounter with Jim is evocative of Darwin, her nurturing behavior after Jim's brutishness is also reminiscent of Ellis's notions regarding the transcendent quality of sexual relations. Although Ellis agrees with Darwin's theory that men and women mate instinctively, he insists that "[w]e are ruled not only by natural instincts but by inherited traditions" (*Studies in the Psychology of Sex, Vol. II*, Part III 178), in this case, the inherited tradition of mothering. Even though Jim's brutishness has made her weep, Liz cannot overcome her traditional female role as nurturer, and the story ends with her tending to Jim's sleeping body by covering him from the cold.

As Hemingway was busy writing these early short stories and perfecting his simple style, he and Hadley were also busy making the acquaintance of numerous modern writers such as the increasingly influential Ezra Pound. Although initially put off by Pound's pretentious demeanor, it was he who first published Hemingway in *The Little Review* and who also acted as Hemingway's first foreign critic, reading Hemingway's poems and commenting on them seriously. Hemingway took Pound's literary advice, just as he did much of Gertrude Stein's when she read the manuscript of his first novel. He ignored, however, her remarks that "Up in Michigan" was unprintable, and sought to publish it, anyway. Stein's disapproval of "Up in Michigan" left such an impression on Hemingway that he felt the need to document it in his semi-autobiographical work, *A Moveable Feast*. Hemingway quotes Stein in the novel:

> 'It's good," she said. "That's not the question at all. But it is inaccrochable. That means it is like a picture that a painter paints and then he cannot hang it when he has a show and nobody will buy it because they cannot hang it either.' (15)

Hemingway says a great deal about Gertrude Stein in *A Moveable Feast*, citing her as a source of knowledge regarding art and literature, and above all, a source of great conversation. One of the talks with Stein which Hemingway chronicles is about sex, and the discussion is perhaps one of Hemingway's examination of homosexuality. In the course of the discussion, Stein declares that Hemingway is too uneducated about sex to understand homosexuality. Hemingway explains that he knows enough about it to feel the need to protect himself around tramps and other dissollutes. Stein tries to explain, however, that not all homosexuals have evil intentions, declaring that Hemingway was "living in a milieu of criminals and perverts" (*A Moveable Feast* 19).

After much discussion, Stein seems to agree with Hemingway's analysis of male homosexuality as frightening, for she declares it to be "ugly and repugnant" (20), and proceeds to proclaim how lesbianism is just "the opposite" 20). Following their conversation, Hemingway leaves feeling "sad" because "[t]he day had started out so brightly" (20). Contemplating the complexity of sexuality and indeed, the complexity of modern life in general, Hemingway cynically muses, "[w]ork could cure almost anything. I believed then, and I believe now. Then all I had to be cured of, I decided Miss Stein felt, was youth and loving my wife" (*A Moveable Feast* 21). While keeping in mind Hemingway's tendency to "dress up" or fictionalize events, there is little doubt that Hemingway did have discussions regarding sex and numerous other matters with Gertrude Stein, as he became a particular favorite of hers and had an open invitation to call. Discussions such as those chronicled in the novel reveal Hemingway's willingness to try to understand homosexuality, to explain his view of it as antithetical to the law of nature, and to possibly be argued out of his fear of it, a fear linked directly to his childhood as discussed in Chapter Three.

His statements in the book regarding a "writing cure" are also remarkable, both for their resemblance to the writing cure attempted by H.D. as advocated by Freud, and also for the candidness of Hemingway's admission that much of "this modern life" required a cure. As with H.D., Hemingway's sexual identity and his identity as a writer are tightly bound. Passages such as this one from *A Moveable Feast* which discuss sex, marriage, writing, and modern ennui, are incredibly common in the works of both writers. While this passage is important evidence of Hemingway's self-acknowledged homophobia, perhaps even more important is Hemingway's contemplation of Stein's remark regarding the necessity of his being "cured" of loving his wife. Unfortunately, Hemingway would indeed be cured of his love for Hadley and would in fact be unable to maintain a stable and monogamous relationship for longer than a few years the rest of his life. Tellingly, Hemingway would divorce Hadley in 1926.

While Stein's insight into the texts produced by numerous moderns was very great, her insight into their personalities was often greater. In *Everybody's Autobiography*, Stein wrote,

> The men all write about themselves, they are always themselves as strong or weak or mysterious or passionate or drunk or controlled but always themselves as the women used to do in the nineteenth century. Now you yourself always do it now why is it. He said it's simple. In the nineteenth century men were confident, the women were not but in the twentieth century the men have no confidence and so they have to

make themselves as you say more beautiful more intriguing more everything and they cannot make any other man because they have to hold on to themselves not having any confidence. (5)

Although actually addressing Dashiell Hammett, this conversation could well describe the struggle for identity experienced by the young Hemingway. Feeling his way for a direct and declarative style often left the writer frustrated and unhappy; it is little wonder that Hemingway is often regarded as behaving boorishly in the early 1920s, for as Stein notes, having no confidence, perhaps the young writer had to make himself seem "more beautiful" and "more intriguing." Certainly the poverty in which he and Hadley lived did nothing to assuage his fears of failure; although working as a correspondent for the *Toronto Star* added a small sum to the Hemingway's income, the varied foreign assignments were far more important in their impact on Hemingway's national sympathies and political ideology.

In particular, his assignment to the Economic Conference in Genoa greatly influenced Hemingway's politics; Stephen Cooper, Kenneth Lynn, and Carlos Baker all cite Hemingway's coverage of the conference as crucially important to the writer's political development. Although initially Hemingway's criticisms of the statesmen present at the conference amounted to little more than caricatures, fifteen newspaper articles later, Hemingway was displaying much keener insight into a conference "of great interest" to him (Baker 89). His experiences covering the Economic Conference renewed Hemingway's interest in political ideologies, an interest so critically damaged by WWI.

Although Hemingway's return to Europe had begun as a sort of writing excursion and second honeymoon for he and Hadley, expatriation to Europe became a crucial element in his development both as a person, and as a writer. Revisiting many of the places which had meant so much to him during WWI, Hemingway realized that both the places and the young man who had been there in 1919 were gone, as was the sense of nationalism and moral duty that sent him to Europe in the first place. His involvement with other expatriate American moderns who were all struggling with the questions of what life was and why it was so directly influenced the presentation of these questions in his own work. Like them, Hemingway was exploring a new form of art which would be more evocative of the modern era.

Hemingway's explorations with prose mirrored his explorations with ideologies, both political and sexual. Reading Darwin and Ellis, Hemingway must also have been aware of Freud, for the sexual promiscuity that arose in response to Freud's theories of repression could not be ignored. Disapproving of Freud, even while apparently suffering from several of the fixations Freud so clearly articulated, Hemingway sought to form his own sexual philosophy in the arms of wife Hadley. Although the relationship failed, Hemingway would continue to explore this sexual philosophy through a series of marriages, optimistically hoping each time that this would be the one which would last. This exploration would culminate in the creation of his longest and most complex novel.

CHAPTER SIX

Catherine (Re)Bourne:
Erotic Symbolism in *The Garden of Eden*

> Catherine was not his enemy except as she was himself in the unfinding unrealizable quest that is love and so was her own enemy.
> —Ernest Hemingway

In the Hemingway canon there are numerous female characters who possess androgynous characteristics or who appear to behave in a manner normally associated with men: Lady Brett Ashley, who can drink and carouse with the other "chaps" in *The Sun Also Rises*; Pilar, the backbone of the armed resistance in *For Whom the Bell Tolls*; and Catherine Bourne, sometime sexual dominatrix and erotic explorer in *The Garden of Eden*. Hemingway often privileges these characters by presenting them in a much more favorable or sympathetic light than their male counterparts. Not surprisingly, Hemingway's real-life female partners would often display androgynous or "masculine" characteristics, reinforcing the idea that for Hemingway, androgyny or at least, the possession of androgynous characteristics, was a positive attribute. It was also a negative one, however, for as we shall see, Hemingway would forever view androgyny as both an asset and a threat.

The Garden of Eden is the most acute example of Hemingway's interest in androgynous women; the creation of Catherine Bourne results in Hemingway's most outstanding female character. E.L. Doctorow asserts that

> [t]here has not before been a female character who so dominates a Hemingway narrative. Catherine in fact may be the most impressive of any woman character in Hemingway's work, more substantive and dimensional than Pilar in *For Whom the Bell Tolls*, or Brett Ashley in *The Sun Also Rises*. Even though she is launched from the naïve premise that sexual fantasizing is a form of madness, she takes on the stature of the self-tortured Faustian, and is portrayed as a brilliant woman trapped into a vicarious participation in someone else's creativity. ("Braver Than We Thought" 44-45)

As Doctorow notes, Catherine Bourne seems larger and more three-dimensional than any previous Hemingway female. The Faustian analogy is particularly definitive of Catherine, for Hemingway's character is a fascinating mixture of good and evil, torturer and tortured, lover and jealous demon. She embodies Hemingway's examination of the complexity of sex and gender, their importance to the creation and recreation of identity, and the ultimate self-destruction that can occur when the line is crossed between desire and obsession. With this chapter, I argue that Hemingway's portrayal of Catherine is so effective because in her, the author fuses Darwin's theories of natural and sexual selection with Ellis's ideas regarding erotic symbolism to explore his own sexual nature and to expound his own philosophy of love. And while Catherine Bourne is arguably a synthesis of many women in Hemingway's life, she is also, as articulated in the epigraph above, an aspect of the author himself.

Although one sexual theory may present itself in a greater preponderance in both Catherine and the novel she inhabits, as noted in my introduction, important to an understanding of sexual theories is the recognition that the ideas presented by Darwin, Ellis, and Freud often overlap. Though I discuss scientific and psychological theories separately, underlying this discussion is the knowledge of sexual theories as engagements of dynamic theoretical discourses, rather than as consistently separate entities.

The most evident sexual theory in *The Garden of Eden* is the transformative fetishizing process Ellis describes in *Erotic Symbolism*. In his work, Ellis accounts for the fetishistic sexual behavior of men and women with a psychological, rather than strictly biological, explanation which had at its roots the idea that an overabundance of sexual love is often the cause of sexual fixation. Ellis's lengthy explanation of erotic symbolism is worth quoting because it summarizes so much that is relevant here:

> By 'erotic symbolism' I mean that tendency whereby the lover's attention is diverted from the central focus of sexual attraction to some object or process which is on the periphery of that focus, or is even outside of it altogether, though recalling it by association of contiguity or of similarity . . . The attractive characteristics of a beloved woman or man, from the point of view of sexual selection, are a complex but harmonious whole leading up to a desire for the complete possession of the person who displays them. (1)

The "desire for . . . complete possession" is precisely the situation with Catherine Bourne in Hemingway's novel. But, although Hemingway was fascinated by Ellis's ideas and case studies, incorporating them in his creation of sexually ambiguous, fixated, and dysfunctional characters, he was nevertheless not completely convinced by Ellis's ideas of sexual transcendentalism in the face of the biological explanations of Darwin. It would appear that while Hemingway may have desired to believe wholeheartedly in Ellis's elevated ideas, his personal experience, his exposure to scientific theory, and his fascination with the male's role in sexual behavior left him capable of incorporating only some of Ellis's ideas and rejecting the rest when creating his own sexual philosophy. As Bert Bender explains,

> It seems probable that Hemingway would have been fascinated, like any other would-be sexual athlete in the years surrounding World War I, with Ellis's analysis of the sexual impulse . . . [B]ut Hemingway soon rejected Ellis's transformation of Darwinian sexual selection (particularly in his volume, *Sexual Selection in Man*) into a religion or art of love. (29)

While it seems apparent that Hemingway rejected many of Ellis's ideas, the sexologist's explanation for anomalous sexual behaviors would forever influence Hemingway's presentation of sexually ambivalent or dysfunctional characters and this influence is nowhere more keenly displayed than in the text of *The Garden of Eden*. The novel that occupied much of Hemingway's time for over ten years blends Darwin's theories of natural and sexual selection with Ellis's explanation of erotically symbolic behavior. Add to this theoretical blending Hemingway's integration of his personal experience with his mother's "emasculating" behavior toward him as a child, as well as the underlying fear of lost masculinity at the root of his desire to leave home, and the notions of androgyny, castration and sexually obsessive behavior become inextricably bound.

Hemingway's love for his mother, as well as his contempt for her dominance, manifests itself in an unending fascination for androgynous and often nearly masculine women, for his fiction, like his personal life, is filled with them. Hemingway's tendency to conflate personal life with fiction is particularly acute in *The Garden of Eden* for his characterization of Catherine Bourne seems to a great degree modeled on his mother and numerous other important women in his life whom he found both admirable and frightening.

Catherine Bourne, like Grace Hemingway, possesses characteristics both compelling and repulsive; even as she attempts to love, the intensity of her feelings pose an emasculating threat for one who is the object of such intense desire. Catherine's androgynous tendencies, illustrated through her athletic prowess (swimming, biking, walking) and her intellectual capacity, coincide closely with many of Grace Hemingway's own traits; they also mirror Ellis's recognition of the relationship between inverted or androgynous behavior and intellectual and physical prowess.

It appears that Hemingway outwardly viewed androgyny itself as quite natural in light of Darwin's theory that human ancestry can be traced to a primordial androgynous organism. As Sulloway points out, this belief was common among sexologists and to them, "the idea of constitutional bisexuality provided one of the most promising solutions to the enigmas of homosexuality and other forms of psychosexual hermaphroditism" (*Freud: Biologist of the Mind* 159).

Nevertheless, it seems likely that Hemingway's early experience dressed as twin to sister Marcelline, as well as the overbearing nature of his mother, left underlying misgivings toward women possessing "masculine" strengths or tendencies. Hemingway's "positive-negative" feelings for androgynous women resulted in a lifelong examination of androgyny, which manifested itself in the creation of female characters unlike any who had previously occupied American fiction. The author's preoccupation with androgyny produced fascinating results, for his most memorable characters, among them Brett Ashley in *The Sun Also Rises,* Pilar and Maria in *For Whom the Bell Tolls,* and of course, Catherine Bourne in *The Garden of Eden,* all display numerous gender characteristics previously assigned to men.

In *The Garden of Eden,* David and Catherine Bourne are a young married couple spending an extended vacation on the Cote d'Azur As the story opens, David and Catherine appear to be leading an idyllic existence which revolves around fishing, eating, and having sexual intercourse. These acts of killing, eating, and having sex occur frequently in the novel, closely following the pattern of previous Hemingway novels, in particular, *The Sun Also Rises.* It is notable that one of the first scenes in the novel revolves around David's catch of a large and beautiful sea bass. This fishing success immediately establishes David as a desirable male in accordance with Darwin's theory of sexual selection, which establishes the female as responsible for choosing her male partner and further states that

> The females are most excited by, or prefer pairing with, the more ornamental males, or those which are the best songsters, or play the best antics; but it is obviously probable that they would at the same time prefer the more vigorous and lively males . . . the most vigorous females . . . will select those which are vigorous and well armed, and in other respects, the most attractive. (*The Descent of Man* 573)

Closely following the fishing scene displaying David's prowess and sexual desirability is another which illustrates Catherine's selection of him as sexual partner as she lies in bed naked, awaiting David's entrance. Catherine not only desires David but takes the sexual initiative by planning a tryst. From the opening of the novel, it is Catherine who wields the sexual power to select and David who exhibits the traits most likely to attract, strong evidence of Hemingway's awareness of the Darwinian sexual reality.

While this heavy emphasis on killing, eating, and sexual intercourse establishes evidence of Hemingway's knowledge of Charles Darwin, the idea of Catherine's need for sexual experimentation, along with several other recurring sexual motifs in the novel, such as a desire to replicate the beloved's physical appearance, also illustrate the author's incorporation of Havelock Ellis's theories regarding sexual obsession and erotic symbolism. The fetishistic or symbolizing process begins early in the novel, three weeks after Catherine and David's marriage, as Catherine immediately develops an obsession with her hair. This obsession is one Hemingway shared. Biographer Carlos Baker describes Hemingway's preoccupation with hair and cites Mary Hemingway's assertion that Hemingway's "interest in the sexual connotations of hair was all the greater because he thought it the one part of a woman's anatomy that could be changed for fun and without permanent damage" (*Ernest Hemingway: A Life Story* 646).

The idea of altering one's appearance as being "fun" is precisely the way Catherine Bourne explains her desire for change, the novel belies this lighthearted explanation and seems more in keeping with other, more sinister, remarks made by Hemingway's last wife. Biographer Kenneth Lynn describes the hair fetish as potentially developing out of an early insistence by Grace Hemingway that the "twins" Marcelline and Ernest would have been even more beautiful if their hair had remained its childish blond. "[H]er repeated extollings of the beauties of blondness had a lasting influence on both children, particularly on Ernest" (*Hemingway* 42). Lynn further reports that

> it would remain for his fourth wife, Mary, to provide the most suggestive indication of how powerfully he had been affected by his mother's views. Some months before their marriage, Mary relates in her autobiography, Ernest persuaded her to ask a hairdresser in Havana to change the color of her hair from peanut butter to platinum. 'I submitted to the bleaching, and Ernest was entranced by the result. Deeply rooted in his field of esthetics was some mystical devotion to blondness, the blonder the lovelier, I never learned why.' (Lynn 42)

Had Mary Hemingway been aware of Grace's preference for blonds and added to this a reading of Ellis' *Erotic Symbolism*, Catherine Bourne's identity as, in part, an extension of Hemingway's own would have revealed his motivation for the bleaching treatment. The bleaching Catherine undergoes is described nearly identically as is Mary's, for not content to be merely blond, Catherine must have hair that is nearly white. In perhaps the most boldly autobiographical move of his life, Hemingway imbeds his own fetishization of hair into a *female* character and then uses her to articulate his explorations of androgyny, homosexuality, and gender. The basis for his obsession is, of course, his mother and his persistent desire for approval. Strangely, though, while the bleaching evinces a desire to be what Grace wants is coupled with the cutting of hair over and over again. If we read this cutting through Freud's theoretical lens, it is representative of emasculation or castration. Seemingly, even while seeking her approval, Hemingway knows, ultimately, that Grace will never be satisfied and will attempt to usurp his masculinity. If we subscribe to this belief, it isn't difficult to connect the David character as the "other," male version of Hemingway.

The first example of Catherine's obsession occurs early in the novel, shortly after the Bourne's arrival in France. With an air of secrecy,

Catherine tells David at breakfast one morning that she is going to surprise him, and then, after a mysterious trip to Aigues Mortes, she meets David at the café with her hair, once long and luxurious, "cropped as short as a boy's" (*The Garden of Eden* 15). Though David seems surprised, he is not displeased as Catherine teases him about the growing similarity of their appearance; this similarity is achieved not merely with the short haircut, but also with Catherine's increasing tendency to wear "masculine" slacks and shirts.

Although the boy's haircut provokes an immediate interpretation of Catherine's desire to become "a boy," a closer reading of this and following scenes reveals that it is not simply androgyny or even transsexualism which Catherine desires. Instead, her behavior is more evocative of erotic obsession, for it is specifically David whom Catherine wishes to resemble. She increasingly desires a sort of "twinship" with David, and this aspect of Hemingway's presentation of erotic obsession is eerily reminiscent of Grace Hemingway's own "smothering" affection for him and her desire to twin him with sister Marcelline. It seems likely that Hemingway felt some anxiety or residual resentment regarding this "twinship" with his sister, considering the possible feminization or emasculation this transgendered experience could have caused. The text of *The Garden of Eden* could arguably be an examination of this anxiety, for the eventual result of erotic obsession is the complete eradication of the love object. The "problem" in *The Garden of Eden* becomes in part, the possible loss of identity suffered not only by Catherine and David Bourne, but potentially by Hemingway himself.

As the novel progresses, the manifestations of Catherine's androgynous tendencies shift from playful sexual explorations into something infinitely more problematic, and it becomes abundantly clear that Catherine's erotic desires run far deeper than mere androgyny. Increasingly demanding and sexually adventurous, Catherine's behavior changes from playful to pathological very quickly.

Her desire to change her appearance begins innocently enough with her insistence that both she and David get their hair cut and dyed the same way. Although David initially resists Catherine's requests, he eventually gives in to her desires:

"Please make it the same as mine," Catherine said.
"But shorter," David said.
"No. Please just the same."

When it was cut David stood up and ran his hand over his head. It felt cool and comfortable. "Aren't you going to let him lighten it?"

"No. We've had enough miracles for one day."
"Just a little?"
"No."

David looked at Catherine and then at his own face in the mirror. His
was as brown as hers and it was her haircut.
"You really want it that much?"
"Yes I do, David. Truly. Just to try it a little bit. Please." (81-82)

David gives in to Catherine's wish for them to look the same, setting a pattern of behavior which becomes difficult for him to break, and which, unfortunately, feeds directly into Catherine's desire to fetishize him. In keeping with Ellis's theory of the extreme case of erotic fetishism, Catherine's erotic obsession with the ideal of David becomes increasingly strong, and soon, no longer content to merely look and act like David, Catherine wishes to *be* David. A foreshadowing of her desire to metamorphose into David occurs earlier in the novel when Catherine expresses her desire for David to play the "role" of Catherine in bed, allowing her to play the male role he normally occupies. While these experiments in sexual positions are most certainly examples of breaks with accepted social custom, they are more importantly, potential textual examples of Hemingway's reading of Ellis's *Erotic Symbolism*.

Occupying the superior or masculine position in bed, Catherine instructs David to call her "Peter," an obvious euphemism for the penis. If the scene stopped with Catherine's instructions for David to be a girl, this transgendered role-playing could illustrate a simple desire to be a boy; however, Catherine does not simply instruct David to be a girl, he must instead be Catherine, David's wife.

"Now you can't tell who is who can you?"
"No."
"You are changing," she said. "Oh you are. You are. Yes you are and you're my girl Catherine" (17).

Mark Spilka views the exchange between David and Catherine as a clear reference to Hemingway's relationship with Pauline Pfeiffer, as does Hemingway biographer Kenneth Lynn, who notes the compelling similarities in the textual and actual relationships:

While walking naked on deserted stretches of beach, the newlyweds also developed their tans, which they further augmented one day by staining their faces with berry juice, for they had decided to bicycle to a local festival disguised as gypsies. In their costumes they looked surprisingly like blood relatives, and two decades later the lingering memory of that family resemblance would inspire Hemingway to set the opening episodes of his strange novel of sexual transference, *The Garden of Eden*, in Le Grau-du-Roi. (363)

As Lynn notes, Pfeiffer and Hemingway displayed many of the tendencies replayed by Catherine and David Bourne; the similarities between life and text are striking. However, Pfeiffer's relationship with Hemingway, like that of his mother, is only partially responsible for this most complex of

Hemingway's novels. More philosophical and psychological exploration than autobiography, *The Garden of Eden* is an intriguing study of Hemingway's interpretation of contemporary sexual theories.

Comley and Scholes point out that the sexually deviant behavior Catherine displays in the novel is damnable, for "in Hemingway's garden the women follow Eve's pattern, seeking forbidden knowledge" (59). Although Comley and Scholes' argument is compelling in the face of David Bourne's nickname for Catherine, "Devil," it appears that any reference to the Christian mythos is ironic and has far less to do with Catherine and David's sexual experimentation than does Hemingway's meditation on what Ellis refers to as "perversion," or the notion of taking sexual exploration too far (a distinctly different definition of perversion than Freud's).

Catherine's progression from simply looking like David and acting like David to becoming David in her erotically symbolic behavior illustrates Hemingway's acceptance of erotic symbolism and fetishism as a form of perversion in the Ellisian sense. Her intense love for David, while initially manifesting itself normally, becomes obsessive and her actions take on the aspect of the actual pervert.

Catherine's obsessive behavior in the novel is not restricted to her actions toward David, however, for even as she is preoccupied with David's image, she is also preoccupied with her own. Catherine's fondness for examining herself in mirrors is evidence of her self-absorption, and mirror imagery increases as her sexual obsession becomes more and more pronounced. It appears that while Hemingway is most obviously employing Ellis's theory of erotic symbolism, the writer's use of mirror imagery implies a conflation of erotic symbolism with Freud's theories of narcissism, for Catherine's fascination with gazing at her "love interest," is an example of both self-love and object-love. As Freud explains, "[t]he state of being in love, so remarkable psychologically, and the normal prototype of psychoses, corresponds to the highest stage of these emanations, in contrast to the state of self-love" (*The Basic Writings of Sigmund Freud* 876). Seemingly, Catherine is caught between "being in love" and being a psychotic. Her obsession with David compels her to behave in a manner not unlike the complete narcissist; she is so insistent on her desire to be David, she must seek affirmation in every mirror she passes. It is the extremity of her love for David which is at the root of Catherine's obsession, a point consistent with both Freud and Ellis.

Once Catherine's sexual obsession is complete, resulting in what Ellis would term an erotic transformation or complete perversion, David has virtually ceased to hold meaning for her as a person. Instead he has become secondary to her erotic obsession with the ideal of being him, or possibly that he has now become a mere reflection of Catherine *as* David. Ellis explains this progressive tendency with regard to erotic symbolism; his discussion of the behavior and explanation for it are crucial to understanding why Hemingway created the Catherine character in the manner he did:

A more nervously exceptional person when once such a symbolism has become firmly implanted, may find it an absolutely essential element in the charm of a beloved and charming person. Finally, for the individual who is thoroughly unsound the symbol becomes generalized; a person is no longer desired at all, being merely regarded as an appendage of the symbol, or being dispensed with altogether; the symbol is alone desired, and is fully adequate to impart by itself complete sexual gratification. While it must be considered a morbid state to demand a symbol as an almost essential part of the charm of a desired person, it is only in the final condition, in which the symbol becomes all-sufficing, that we have a true and complete perversion. (30)

Hemingway portrays Catherine in just such an exceptionally nervous manner, high-strung and unpredictable, that is, as exhibiting the classic symptoms of the "unsound" character Ellis describes. By the time Catherine brings home Marita as both lesbian lover and a partner for David, her erotically symbolic transformation is achieved, and she has finally succeeded in becoming him, albeit temporarily.

In Catherine's mind, the shared possession of Marita is the culmination of her symbolic transformation into David, or at least, David's double. It isn't an easy transformation, however, for the realization that she will have to share David isn't as pleasant as the theorizing; also, previous to the affair with Marita, Catherine has not had sex with a woman and has no real sense of what to do. The problems with realizing her erotic goal become very clear when David, Catherine and Marita are having drinks. Marita tries to salvage the tense situation between the three of them and begins a conversation:

> "I like my present. Did someone take my drink?"
> "I threw it out," Catherine said. "David will make a new one."
> "I hope you still like having two girls," she said. "Because I am yours and I'm going to be Catherine's too."
> "I don't go in for girls," Catherine said. It was very quiet and her voice didn't sound right either to herself or to David.
> "Don't you ever?"
> "I never have."
> "I can be your girl, if you ever want one, and David's, too."
> "Don't you think that's a vast undertaking?" Catherine asked. (105)

The "vast undertaking" appears to be both the necessity of sexually educating Catherine and presumably also sexually satisfying both Catherine and David, which Marita initially attempts to do.

The situation quickly unravels, however, for as Catherine realizes, her transformation into David is merely a symbolic one; ultimately, although she may dress like him, look like him, and like him, have sex with a woman, Catherine can never do the one thing that essentially comprises David's authentic self. She cannot write. The implications that this will be a problem run throughout the text, beginning with Catherine's obvious jealousy regarding the newspaper clippings and her continued jealousy of the time David spends writing. Catherine's final realization that she cannot be "David the writer" leads to the most shocking scene in the book, in which David realizes she has burned the African stories as well as the newspaper clippings of his success.

Burning the evidence of David's talent is Catherine's last attempt at maintaining her delusion or retaining her symbolic identity as David or his double. When she reads the stories and realizes how much of his identity is intertwined with both what David writes and the act of writing itself, Catherine lashes out and destroys the evidence of her inability to maintain her identity as David. At this point in the published text, Catherine's mental health crumbles, as does her marriage. She departs the hotel leaving David and Marita to presumably live happily ever after. It might be argued that Catherine's departure at the end of the novel is Hemingway's way of "punishing" her for breaking cultural taboos or if she is in fact partly representational of his mother, punishing Grace; it could also be his way of warning anyone of the potential danger of drifting too far from his or her own ultimate biological role. However, Hemingway's unedited manuscript does not end with Catherine's departure.

In his provisional ending to the novel, Hemingway has Catherine and David reunited and as they did long ago, they are lying on the beach. This coming together at the end of the novel negates any possibility that Catherine must be punished for her obsessive behavior, and it also radically departs from any "real life" Hemingway relationships, for it was the author's tendency to make clean and final his breaks with former wives. The provisional ending reveals the possibility that Hemingway considered Ellis's description of the erotically symbolic condition as curable, which was often the case. His depiction of Catherine as reunited with David could also be evidence of Hemingway's belief that men and women, although often sidetracked by the sexual complexity of modern life, should ultimately maintain their biological purpose.

This idea is reinforced in another Hemingway work which addresses sexual transformation, "The Sea Change." In the story, Ernest Hemingway weaves a story around the death of love, or, if not love, at least the death of an intimate relationship. This story is unusual because unlike other Hemingway tales, such as "Hills Like White Elephants" or "Cat in the Rain" which seem to center around the inability of men and women to truly communicate, it is not precisely a problem within the young couple's relationship that causes their unhappiness. Instead, it is the onset of the woman's desire for a sexual relationship with another woman that brings their love affair to an end. Also, as with most of Hemingway's works, the title's implication plays an important role as the site of, or catalyst for, the "change" that ultimately overcomes the couple's relationship.

In the story, Hemingway presents the couples' situation primarily through dialogue, rather than narration. The use of dialogue is one of the author's great achievements in his manipulation of the short story as a genre. The ability to seemingly telescope an entire chain of events (i.e., everything that led up to the breakup) and relate them to the reader through short, clipped conversations, is nowhere more evident than in this short story. Although the reader must make certain assumptions about the state of affairs between the two characters prior to the beginning of the story (like most of the short stories, the tale begins with a situation that is in medias res), very little work is required to ascertain the narrative thread. For example, the opening lines of "The Sea Change" do much to set both the emotional scene and clue the reader toward the nature of the conflict:

> "All right," said the man. "What about it?"
> "No," said the girl, "I can't."
> "You mean that you won't."
> "All right," said the girl, "You have it your own way."
> "I don't have it my own way. I wish to God I did."
> "You did for a long time," the girl said.
> (*The Complete Short Stories*, 302)

From this brief exchange, the reader already knows that the man has made an important request of the girl with which she feels unable to comply. Also, there is a strong hint that their relationship has been ongoing and intimate for some time, but that now because of an as yet undisclosed outside force, the nature of their relationship has changed. Not only is the man anguished (wishing to God), but also, it is obvious that he is so because of a shift of power (no longer having his own way), a shift that has left him the loser. Although as yet the reader is not sure exactly who or what has been lost, it is evident that the nature of the loss is grave enough to warrant this concern.

Directly following this conversation is one full paragraph of narration. (There are only four such in the entire story. The remaining narration consists of a few lines here and there.) In the first narrative paragraph, Hemingway provides the reader with several crucial pieces of information. The first is that the story takes place at the end of the summer. Considering the title and the narrator's remark that "they were both tanned, so that they looked out of place in Paris," the reader is cued that the couple have recently returned from a summer trip to the seaside, possibly a resort on the coast of France. Also, as the reader further considers the remark that "they were *both* tanned" and links it to the remaining description of the girl ("The girl wore a tweed suit, her skin was a smooth golden brown, her blonde hair was cut short"), the reader realizes that the author has presented her as rather androgynous. Although Hemingway describes her as beautiful, the reader is suspect, for it is not a distinctly feminine beauty which he describes. The rather masculine appearance ascribed to the girl seems unimportant; however, when the reader considers her in the light of the time of the story's publication in the twenties, a decade during which androgyny and lesbianism were closely linked, the description takes on far greater import in the Hemingway story. As Lillian Faderman points out in her work on the evolution of lesbianism in America, the 1920's had a "preoccupation with androgyny" (*Odd Girls and Twilight Lovers* 102).

As the dialogue resumes with "I'll kill her," and continues with lines like, "If it was a man—," and fulminates with the man's remark, "Perversion," the reader is rewarded for picking up on Hemingway's cues with regard to the girl. It becomes clear that the source of conflict between the couple is another woman. Continuing this line of dialogue, Hemingway reveals the man's insistence on clarifying that this desire is somehow very wrong. The girl, however, tries to refute any sense of wrongdoing by rejecting his label of perversion.

> "I'd like it better if you didn't use words like that," the girl said.
> "There's no necessity to use words like that."
> "What do you want me to call it?"
> "You don't have to call it. You don't have to put any name to it."
> "That's the name for it"
> "No," she said. "We're made up of all sorts of things. You've known that. You've used it well enough." (*The Complete Short Stories* 304)

The idea that humans are "made up of all sorts of things" is important in deciphering just what the struggle is all about between these two, for if the girl was *only* lesbian, there would really be no need for discussion. She would simply leave the man. Instead, the conflict between them centers around the idea that she has both a love or desire for the man, and also, a desire to be with someone of her own sex. Also, this line of dialogue implies that the man has had some shortcomings in the past for which he has also used this same excuse or explanation ("You've known that. You've used it well enough."). Eventually, however, even the girl admits that what she desires is "all wrong," but she still persists in her wish to leave and resents the man for wishing to restrain her. She wants his permission to go and implies that if he allows it, she will return:

> "You mean all wrong. I know. It's all wrong. But I'll come back. I told you I'd come back. I'll come back right away."
> "No, you won't."
> "I'll come back."
> "No, you won't. Not to me."
> "You'll see."
> "Yes," he said. "That's the hell of it. You probably will."
> (*The Complete Short Stories* 304)

As the conversation between them continues, it is clear to the reader that the man is defeated. He cannot restrain the girl from leaving, even though he knows that she will return. He gives his consent, and she departs. What is perhaps most crucial to the story, however, is not directly stated either by dialogue or through narration. It is the question of *why* both the man and the girl insist that she will return. Deeply embedded in the story is the notion that biologically, men and women have a bisexual genetic makeup ("We're made up of all sorts of things"), but that bisexuality is not our ultimate orientation. Only through heterosexuality can men and women fulfill their biological function and reproduce offspring. This is natural or right, to Hemingway, and deviation from our natural purpose is, indeed, perversion. Although the potential for homosexuality or bisexuality lies within, it is not ultimately fulfilling, and so, the girl must return.

In this light, the sea as background becomes so important. It is in the sea that all natural life, all biological creatures, are born. It is potentially there, also, that deviations, mutations, or possibly new creations, are made. The sea is the site of natural change. Conversely, in the story, the sea has been the site of an unnatural change, at least in the girl. It would appear, however, that her change is only a temporary one, that she will eventually return and find her rightful biological place. The change wreaked on the man, however, appears permanent, for in the final scene of the story, the man gazes at himself in the mirror and his appearance has altered. Although the bartender says he looks well, the man has changed, and he seems to feel that it is not for the better.

There are several ways to interpret this visible alteration in the man's appearance, dependent upon to whom the reader assumes he is directing the statement regarding vice. "Vice, " said the brown young man, "is a very strange thing, James" (*The Complete Short Stories* 305). Although the man had earlier quoted on vice to the girl with regard to her perverted behavior, in this scene he could potentially be discussing himself. It is difficult to truly ascertain, but perhaps the man is contemplating his own behavior, either in his rather malicious insistence on labeling the girl's desires, his potential jealousy, or perhaps some unnamed vice which lies within his own breast. When the reader recalls his earlier statement to the girl, "Vice is a monster of such fearful mien," the young man said bitterly, "that to be something or other needs but to be seen. Then we something, something, then embrace," it is difficult to avoid criticizing the man for his cold behavior toward the girl. There was certainly no "embrace" or forgiveness for her, even though she apologized many times, and this cruelty, although understandable considering his loss, is not condonable. It would appear that his own vices, jealousy, lack of sympathy, and egotism, could have changed his appearance.

In an even less flattering light, Hemingway's character could be commenting that his appearance has altered from being in such close contact with the "vice" of perversion. The least acceptable choice for the reader, for the author has not painted the girl in an unflattering light, which the reader assumes he would have done had he wished to use her as the source of the man's "change." Still, it is not out of the realms of possibility, for as in the scene in the Café Select in *The Sun Also Rises*, Hemingway often treats homosexuals harshly.

"The Sea Change" is complex in its discussion of the human relationship which is the central focus of the story. Although the reader is given many cues regarding the situation, because they are done with dialogue rather than much omniscient narration, the details of the story are fairly ambiguous. It is fair to say that the man is losing the girl over another woman; that can be construed quite clearly. Why he has lost her and what effect that has left is less easy to decipher. The sea as background can be used effectively in understanding the biological subtheme of the story, but on a more metaphoric level, it could be representative of the more enigmatic behavior of men and women. We are changeable creatures; we are "made up of all sorts of things," and often our behavior is inexplicable. Perhaps Hemingway is offering that notion, too, up for scrutiny here by not directly stating the girl's motivations. Perhaps also, that is why he uses so much dialogue in this piece, for dialogue more directly relates language's great incapacity to relate intention. Given, also, that this scene is set in a public place, a bar, it would almost appear as if the couple are fearful of too directly confronting what is at the root of their situation. In a public place, one is less likely to expose the soft inner core of the self; instead, one must follow a certain code of behavior, of politeness. This compounds the ambiguity of the language, because the characters cannot give much voice to the "unspeakable" subject that confounds their relationship. The element of ambiguity with regard to the characters' motivations is perhaps why Hemingway is so effective. Ambiguity, lack of perception, fear of disclosing the inner self's desire for love, all these things occur in his works and in his life.

As I have suggested, Hemingway's articulation of love and sex is a philosophy which is situated "squarely on Darwin's theory of sexual selection" (Bender 342), and which insists on the notion of competition. I argue, however, Hemingway's competitive "game" also heavily borrows from Havelock Ellis's extension of Darwin's theory. The reading of contemporary sexual theories is frequently omitted from any mention of Hemingway's texts, however, and while biographers such as Mark Spilka provide invaluable information about Hemingway's life, they often oversimplify the importance of specific people (such as Grace Hemingway) in the creation of Hemingway's characters. Spilka, who writes a great deal about what Hemingway read, crucially omits any mention of social or scientific works, particularly those produced by Charles Darwin and Havelock Ellis even though the works of both authors occupied substantial space in the Hemingway library. This lack of perception is a common critical oversight which leads to gross misreadings of Hemingway's texts. As

Hemingway was a self-proclaimed natural scientist, it is difficult to understand this critical omission.

Nancy Comley and Robert Scholes move beyond Spilka's explanation of Catherine Bourne as hybrid of Grace Hemingway and Pauline Pffeiffer and shed a great deal of light on Hemingway's interest in androgyny by examining his presentation and criticism of gender and sexuality. They speculate on Hemingway's ideas regarding the cultural construction of gender and the ensuing sex and gender "taboos." Their discussion of *The Garden of Eden* is particularly arresting in its presentation of Catherine as Hemingway's symbolic breaker of cultural constraints and his analysis of the repercussions of such behavior,

> [f]or Catherine Bourne, to experience what boys feel is to transgress, to break a taboo that is not merely social but religious. Such transgression, linked as it is to darkness and damnation, is coded in the Hemingway text as madness. After such knowledge, as T.S. Eliot would put it, 'what forgiveness.' (59)

While their idea that Catherine's madness is the result of sexual transgression seems sound, Comley and Scholes still miss Hemingway's point, for although in the published text Hemingway does, indeed, show Catherine as suffering a sort of mental breakdown, in line with Ellis's theory of the nervous condition suffered by the erotic fetishist, the original manuscript does not finish there. Intent on proving that Hemingway's Eden is built on a Judeo-Christian framework by citing the catastrophes that befall all the characters who break with custom, Comley and Scholes ignore Hemingway's own provisional ending to the novel, an ending which completely discounts any notion of hell and damnation. While there is certainly much to be gleaned from Comley and Scholes reading of the novel, ignoring the provisional ending of the manuscript seems to misrepresent Hemingway's ideas. With the provisional ending, Hemingway, like Ellis, shows that obsessive love while not normal, is certainly human and therefore, forgivable. As Ellis states,

> [e]rotic symbolism is therefore concerned with all that is least generic, least specific, all that is most intimately personal and individual, in sexual selection . . . In the widest and most abstract form of sexual selection in man is merely human, and we are attracted to that which bears most fully the marks of humanity. (107)

Ellis's humane tone seems more reflective of Hemingway's original manuscript than does the more dogmatic one argued by Comley and Scholes, and while *The Garden of Eden*, like other Hemingway novels before it, such as *The Old Man and the Sea*, has many symbols reminiscent of the Christian mythos, in light of Hemingway's agnostic behavior and philosophical searching, as well as his acceptance of Darwin's evolutionary theory, the symbols here seem more ironic than literal. The biblical version of

Eden had only one Eve whose sexuality was unquestionably female and also in the biblical Eden, carnal knowledge was punishable by death. In the Hemingway text, carnal knowledge is not judged, precisely; instead, sexuality is expressive and experimental and only those behaviors which are ultimately non-productive or procreative are put aside. Even if one discounts the provisional ending to the novel, Catherine's madness is explainable in light of contemporary psychological theories, particularly those of Ellis. When one examines the erotic behavior of Catherine and David in *The Garden of Eden*, the presentation of Eden seems far more like a garden witnessed through Darwinian or Ellisian eyes than the eyes of God. Although the novel's title is certainly biblical in origin, the content of the novel seems far more grounded in Darwin's theories of sexual selection and Havelock Ellis's idea regarding sexual fetishism. David's masculinity is constantly linked to his ability to kill and eat, and Catherine's love for him becomes so consuming, so obsessive that by the end of the novel it has quite literally driven her mad. The provisional ending of the novel presents the possibility that David's understanding of Catherine's behavior, as well as his deep love for her, can resolve her sexual fixation. It is interesting that the provisional ending seems evocative of David's forgiveness of Catherine's behavior when we recall her resemblance to Grace Hemingway; while Hemingway may have intended David to forgive Catherine, he himself could never quite forgive his mother.

Bender states that Ellis was important reading for the author as he formed his own view of sexual reality; he also argues, however, that Hemingway "shoulder[ed] aside" Havelock Ellis and another theorist of modern love, Ezra Pound, in presenting his own more Darwinian natural history of love. While Hemingway may "shoulder aside" much of Ellis's philosophy, the psychologist's theoretical imprint is indelibly stamped on much of the author's work. Although Hemingway may have dismissed much of Ellis's sexual philosophy, given the striking resemblance between Catherine's behavior toward David in *The Garden of Eden* and the remarkable case histories of sexual fetishists in Ellis's *Erotic Symbolism*, the fascination for Ellis's theories regarding sexually obsessive behavior seems a plausible creative source for Hemingway's characters.

Interestingly, Ellis's explanation of erotic symbolism maintains that in severe cases of erotic obsession, the mentally ill lover goes beyond fetishism of the loved one. In extreme cases, the lover was ultimately transformed into a replication of the beloved, resulting, in Ellisian terms, in erotic transference or transformation, which is precisely the case with Catherine. Transference or transformation, however, are also terms clearly evocative of another contemporary theorist of human sexuality, Sigmund Freud. Like the mirror imagery in the novel, the notion of transference denotes Freud's influential presence in the novel.

Mark Spilka maintains that the transformation through erotic symbolism in *The Garden of Eden* is actually evidence of Hemingway's reworking of F. Scott Fitzgerald's psychologically disturbing *Tender is the Night*. There are many aspects of the Fitzgerald novel which resurface in Hemingway's text. *Tender is the Night* chronicles the life of a promising young psychoanalyst whose passion for and ultimate marriage to a neurotic patient results in his eventual disintegration and her transformation into a healthy woman. During this transformation process, the Fitzgerald heroine has a lesbian encounter which Spilka refers to as the "lesbian lark." The Fitzgerald novel is a highly autobiographical account of his tormented relationship with wife, Zelda, and her continuing battle for sanity. Fitzgerald employs a great many Freudian symbols and ideas, among them the notion of patient-analyst transference, this time gone seriously awry.

From correspondence between Hemingway and Fitzgerald, it is evident that Hemingway publicly detested how the popularity of Freud had "intellectualized" love, and it could be argued that his reworking of the Fitzgerald novel served as a vehicle for the devaluation of Freud's theories and subsequent presentation of Hemingway's alternative philosophy of love and sex with its roots in Darwin and Ellis. However, Hemingway's public detestation for Freud's theories may simply have acted as a cover for his more private fears regarding their applicability to his own life. Hemingway's unusual upbringing, the "love-hate" relationship with his mother, his consistent preference for male company all may have contributed to a fear of being labeled with one of Freud's increasingly popular "complexes," a fear that may well have proved apropos.

As a man appreciative of male company and male prowess, Hemingway had good cause to fear Freud's theories with their description of the "latency" involving men who felt both compelled to seek out male companions and while in their company, engage in acts of bravado and tests of male virility. Latent homosexuality has been and continues to be an accusation made with regard to Hemingway by numerous critics; however, once apprised of Clarence Hemingway's "frontier" approach to childrearing with its emphasis on physical tests of strength and skill, it seems far more likely that Hemingway's adult behavior had its roots there. Rather than latently homosexual, Hemingway was instead conditioned to compete and enjoyed doing so; his frequent preference for male company lies possibly in the fact that women tended to engage in more "domestic" pursuits which for Hemingway held no interest. His fondness for physical activity, gambling, drinking, and socializing kept him primarily in the company of men and was greatly responsible for the failure of his first marriage. With the birth of Bumby, wife Hadley simply could not keep up; without her, Hemingway continued to live life as he did when single.

It would appear that rather than latently homosexual, Hemingway was simply more comfortable in the company of men, particularly men who like himself, engaged in "manly" activities with "afficion." Because his closest and longest relationships were with men, Hemingway's friendships have often been questioned as more than mere friendships; in light of the work of Freud, it is likely that the author at times may have questioned these relationships himself. However, while Hemingway may have scrutinized his male affiliations, his overwhelmingly negative feelings for homosexuals are well-documented and certainly not uncommon for the times. Accusations of homosexuality were very real threats to masculine identity during the modern era; while androgyny and bisexuality were aspects of identity openly discussed, particularly among women, to be a homosexual male was to be socially emasculated. For Hemingway, his distaste for homosexuality was compounded by his knowledge of biological theories, and unlike his "positive-negative" view of androgyny, he could see no positive side to a lifestyle so "unnatural" in the Darwinian sense. That Hemingway held this view is clear in *The Sun Also Rises* with his dark portrayal of the gay men in the Café Select as men with "white hands, wavy hair, white faces, grimacing . . . I was very angry. Somehow they always made me angry. I know they are supposed to be amusing, and you should be tolerant, but I wanted to swing on one, any one, anything to shatter that superior, simpering posture" (20). Unlike his admiration for the androgynous-looking Brett Ashley (whom Hemingway describes as "damned good-looking"), Hemingway has nothing but fear and contempt for the completely homosexual men. While androgyny may have been a complicated but often positive characteristic, Hemingway seemed to view homosexuals as in denial of there biological selves, either due to a pathology, or psychology. Although he had made attempts at understanding homosexuality (as when he questioned Stein in Paris), Hemingway's feelings toward homosexuals were confused and generally negative.

Hemingway's homophobia can perhaps be explained by Eve Sedgwick who articulates the fear of homosexual labeling in her discussion of "homosexual panic"; she explains that while society insists that men be thrust together daily in a series of "homosocial" activities including work, sports, and the sexual segregation often mandatory at social functions, the homosocial bonds which men form must be close but not intimate. The difficulty of negotiating the "close but not intimate" bonds is at the root of the homosexual panic, for normally when people are engaged in close activities, rife as they are with positive feelings of camaraderie and enjoyment, sexual impulses are likely to surface. However, when the people involved are all male, suddenly these feelings must be rechannelled to prevent the possibility of a homosexual encounter. As Sedgwick articulates it, during "certain intense male bonds that were not readily distinguishable from the most reprobated bonds, an endemic and ineradicable state of what I am calling male homosexual panic became the normal condition of the male heterosexual entitlement" (15). Sedgwick explains that "the continuum of male homosocial bonds has been brutally structured by a "homosexual possibility" in all but the declared homosexual. Fearing homosexual labeling, men like Hemingway who clearly enjoyed the homosocial bonds they so actively sought, often positioned themselves protectively as homophobic, and subsequently, anti-Freudian. The fact remains, however, that postures often lie and there is much in *The Garden of Eden* reminiscent of both Freud and Fitzgerald; because of this, Spilka's assessment of the intertextual relationship between *Tender is the Night* and *The Garden of Eden* seems very possible.

While Spilka credits much of the plot for *The Garden of Eden* to Fitzgerald, he also asserts that the African stories in the novel can be attributed to Hemingway's reading of Rudyard Kipling. Unlike the presence of Fitzgerald, however, this assessment seems to me incorrect. While there is little doubt that Hemingway read and admired Kipling, rather than a reworking of the author, the jungle stories seem more an admittance to the accuracy of Darwin's theories regarding the instinctual necessity to kill and eat than they do a revision of Kipling's work.

Darwin aside, the African stories in *The Garden of Eden* also potentially act as representations of Hemingway's struggle for masculinity and his resolution to break the bonds of his parents' control. By having the boy Davey in the story make ethical choices, some of which directly conflict with those of his domineering father, the African stories appear to replicate, to some degree, Hemingway's own life choices. While his parents desired him to become an educated man, a doctor like his father, Hemingway made the decision to become a writer. His insistence on this matter put to rest any notions of who would be in charge of his destiny and it is a theme played out many times in the short fiction written after Hemingway's return from WWI, as in "Soldier's Home," for example. The sorrow and resentment young Davey feels in the African stories is also reminiscent of the pain Hemingway experienced after continual years of disappointment and disapproval from Grace and Clarence Hemingway. The correspondence between Hemingway and his parents chronicles the disintegration of their relationship while the loss of his father to suicide could only have compounded feelings of pain and sorrow.

The African stories in *The Garden of Eden* are not short fiction, precisely, but are instead brief vignettes of metafiction, for even as they operate as vehicles to illustrate the adult David's growth as a writer, they can also be read as a separate narrative. Whether or not Fitzgerald's *Tender is the Night* inspired Hemingway's posthumous novel, his reading of androgyny in *The Garden of Eden* combines Ellis's ideas regarding female passion and erotic symbolism with Darwin's theories of the predatory nature of men and women. The fusion of these theories with Hemingway's admittance to the shifting nature of sex and gender as illustrated through Catherine and David Bourne resulted in the author's most ambitious novel.

When read autobiographically, *The Garden of Eden* becomes a telling chronicle of Hemingway's experience with androgyny and the complexity of sexual identity; the novel articulates Hemingway's lifelong contemplation of identity and human relationships and elucidates his own philosophy of love. Reading the "Garden" text through sex theories and autobiography dispels any remaining misperceptions of Hemingway as misogynist and explains his homophobia as a protective shield of public and personal scrutiny, illustrating a man trying to come to terms both with himself and his world in the dynamic period we term "the modern era."

CHAPTER SEVEN

"Nebulous" Personalities

> I, a nebulous personality without a name.
> —H.D.

As with Hemingway, H.D.'s protagonists are generally versions of herself, created and recreated situationally in the context of their relationships with others. Susan Friedman uses H.D.'s own metaphor for her creation of self/characters when she describes H.D. as a "Penelope" who in her production of texts is occupying a dual role as both weaver and woven, author and subject. In this dual role, the "woman as writer" is further complicated as she occupies her position as both the object of desire and the one who wants. For H.D., as with all writers, sexuality and gender are inextricably tied to authorship; as Friedman explains, "H.D.'s prose is overwhelmingly centered on the legend of the woman writer for whom the erotic and the linguistic are inseparable" (84).

Even as women write themselves, however, they must also read and this reading is not confined to the female text. Friedman asserts that "[t]he presence of prior reading in women's life-writing includes an interrogation of what men have written about women" (85). Friedman's emphasis on the importance of what women read about themselves in male texts (and subsequently revise and recreate in their own) is crucial to understanding the difficulties women face when attempting to write their lives. Blau DuPlessis also addresses the importance of reading in the construction of women's writing, declaring that

> [i]t is, after all, always the meaning, the reading of difference that matters, and meaning is culturally engendered and sustained. Not to consider the body as some absolute (milk, blood, breasts, clitoris) for no "body" is unmediated. Not body but the "body" of psychosocial fabrication of difference, or again, of sameness, or again, of their relation. ("For the Etruscans" 273)

Blau DuPlessis argues here that in every aspect in life, but particularly, in our cultural recording through writing, women are "written" or created as "different." This expectation of difference constitutes a false construct of the female that women had to deconstruct both in life and in their writing.

In H.D.'s case, the difficulties are compounded, for not only is she "reading" herself and her times through female representations in male literary texts but also through the image of woman presented in the texts of the male sexologists and psychologists. H.D.'s continual rewriting of herself and her contemporaries then becomes a revision of existing literary and theoretical images of woman; she is "re-viewing" herself through the lens of what sexologists assert women to be as well as what literature portrays them to be. Frequently, this revision is achieved by using imagery evocative of the language and ideas of Darwin, Ellis, and Freud.

Much has been said about H.D.'s "weaving and reweaving" of her self and times through the language of sexual theory, the emphasis markedly Freudian. Teresa De Lauretis discusses the importance of Freud's work to the texts of women writer's, particularly lesbian or "women oriented" writers, such as those produced by H.D. De Lauretis discusses "psychoanalysis as a theory of sexuality and sexual difference" and explains that

> [i]f the first feminine emphasis on sexual difference as woman's difference from man has rightly come under attack for obscuring the effects of other differences in women's psychosocial oppression, nevertheless that emphasis on sexual difference did open up a critical space—a conceptual, representational, and erotic space—in which women could address themselves to women. And in the very act of assuming and speaking from the position of subject, a woman could concurrently recognize women as subjects and as objects of female desire. (5)

De Lauretis's point here is to illustrate that even as Freud's theory reinforced many sexually oppressive ideas regarding women, it was also the first step toward women's recognition of the debilitating effects caused by their position as "the second sex." De Lauretis maintains that the small "space" Freud's theory opened allowed women to recognize themselves as sexual beings in both heterosexual and homosexual relationships.

This recognition is perhaps why H.D. critics and the author herself associate psychoanalysis with her work; among others, Claire Buck and Dianne Chisholm apply Freudian theory in their excellent texts on H.D., and their discussions are extremely illuminating. While these critical texts are useful tools in the analysis of H.D. as both poet and novelist, there is much room for elaboration on the author's application of contemporary sex theories in both her creation of character and enumeration of self. This chapter extends the discussion of Freud and H.D. undertaken by feminist critics and also expands the brief mention of Darwin and Ellis. By reading H.D.'s female protagonists through three theoretical lenses, I emphasize H.D.'s incorporation of contemporary sexual theories into her work.

Darwin: Standing in the Margins

> We must consider Darwin's work on the origin of species as the very foundation of a new epoch.
> —Carl Claus

While psychoanalysis is the most popular sexual and psychological lens through which to scrutinize H.D. and her works, text after text on H.D. does so with no mention of Charles Darwin. As stated in the introduction to this work, an acceptance of Darwin is crucial to any psychoanalytic reading, for Darwin's theories of evolution, especially his theory of sexual selection, is the precursor to both Freud's psychoanalytic theory and Ellis's more metaphysical one.

Gillian Beer comments on the "interdisciplinary" importance of evolutionary theory, explaining that "[t]he power of Darwin's writing in his culture is best understood when it is seen not as a single origin or 'source,' but in its shifting relations to other areas of study" (10). As Beer implies, Darwin's theory impacted numerous fields of study, including the work of Freud and his creation of psychoanalysis. It would follow that critical works which examine literary texts through extensive discussion of psychoanalytic theory would mention Darwin. This has not, however, been the case; in fact, little mention is made of Darwin in literary studies whatsoever. Bert Bender attempts to account for this critical oversight, hypothesizing that while there are many reasons for "Darwin's relative absence in American literary history" (*The Descent of Love* 5) there are several which seem most likely. Bender states that

> few literary critics seem to have read Darwin and have therefore incorrectly assumed that his theory was rather simple, after all, and not particularly new; that the crisis of faith that followed Origin of Species was only a culmination of the developing conflict between science and religion that had been under way at least since the Renaissance; that "the survival of the fittest" involves mainly an elaboration on Tennyson's earlier image of "Nature, red in tooth and claw"; that the fascination with nature's brute violence or the environmental forces in social Darwinism is of limited interest and was thoroughly exploited by our rather adolescent naturalists ... in short, that a writer was either a "Darwinist" or not ... (5)

Bender describes the inaccuracy of these perceptions, explaining that "nearly everyone was to some extent a 'Darwinist'" (5) and further that

> writers who sought to present the reality of modern courtship and marriage (particularly the younger ones like Howells and James) were contending with each other — no less than were the biologists and anthropologists, for example — for the right to claim that their own interpretations of life were true to the new evolutionary reality, (5-6)

American authors and critics may not acknowledge Darwin overtly (with the possible exceptions of Kate Chopin and Edith Wharton); nevertheless, the father of evolutionary theory is and has been standing in the margins of the authors' texts, providing the theoretical "white space" wherein each could situate their textual interpretations of life. Although modern authors and their audience were accepting of Darwin's theories, literary history lost sight of his importance, particularly after the excitement over *The Origin of Species* had died down. *The Descent of Man and Selection in Relation to Sex* received far less attention than the preceding work, even while it had "far greater impact" (Bender 7); soon, discussion of Darwin's theories and their import were replaced with discussions of new theorists who had followed.

It is perhaps due to the readability of his texts that Darwin's works were so quickly eclipsed; lacking the expressive and explicit jargon of Freud, Darwin's language was instead, accessible, and perhaps because of that, forgettable. Gillian Beer reminds us of the relatively simple language of Darwin in her examination of his narrative form; however, Beer points out a more important reason for the possible neglect of evolutionary theory. While other theories of creation and human behavior revolve around man, evolutionary theory exhibited a complete "absence of any reference to man as the crowning achievement of the natural and supernatural order" making the text "subversive" (Beer 60). Darwin did not place man and the "here and now" at the center of existence and Beer explains this failure as

> one of the difficulties on the path of evolutionary theory. It is a theory which does not privilege the present, which sees it as a moving instant in an endless process of change. Yet it has persistently been recast to make it seem that all the past has been yearning towards the present moment and is satisfied. (13)

Whatever the reason for Darwin and his theories' eventual omission, my purpose in discussing them here is to emphasize two things. First, in the scientific household in which she grew up, H.D. would have been aware of *The Origin of Species by Means of Natural Selection* and *The Descent of Man and Selection in Relation to Sex*. These texts would have inhabited the same shelves as the works written by her naturalist grandfather and astronomer father. Second, because so much of my discussion in this chapter involves H.D.'s incorporation of the texts of Ellis and Freud, I wish to give credit where it has long been due. Rather than view Darwin as standing in the margins, it seems more accurate to see him in a variety of ways, translated into the printed text of all who would attempt an examination of human behavior. As Sulloway explains,

> When Charles Darwin, in his celebrated book On the Origin of Species (1859), announced to a disbelieving world that the supposed Organic Creation was not creation at all but rather the result of a natural evolutionary process . . . he probably did more than any other

individual to pave the way for Sigmund Freud and the psychoanalytic revolution. (239)

Conspicuous evidence of Darwin's presence in H.D.'s work is relative; more obvious in the poetry, Darwinian language is particularly acute in the *Sea Garden* poems. Published in 1916, *Sea Garden* is a collection of poems Susan Friedman describes as "a sequence of modern pastorals set in a symbolic green world removed from conventional space and time" (51). Friedman argues that "Theocritius, the Hellenistic poet and father of the pastoral, was, significantly, one of H.D.'s earliest models" (51), and goes on to define the pastoral as a genre which "suggests a binary opposition between nature and culture in which the poet is located in an imaginary realm temporarily removed from the confinements of the social order" (51). Friedman's definition of the pastoral seems also applicable to the poet herself, for at the time she created the poems collected in *Sea Garden*, H.D. was caught between nature and culture. Unwilling to completely submit to the social conventions of the times and marry a local boy sensibly, H.D. opted instead to go abroad, leaving a "normal" life to undertake one in a strange, and for her, unknown land. By rejecting the role outlined for most young women of upper-middle class backgrounds, H.D.'s social position became indeterminate. She was now physically removed "from the confinements of the social order," and instead occupied the hazy position of traveler.

However, even as Friedman accurately makes the Hellenistic pastoral connection between H.D. and Theocritus, she admits to the vast difference between H.D.'s "wild and dissonant landscape" and the "harmonious, domesticated nature" of the ancient pastoral poet. Friedman does not attempt to explain or account for this difference or inconsistency, perhaps considering it unimportant to her argument. When discussing the poems in light of H.D.'s exposure to the theories of Charles Darwin, however, the immense difference in tone and imagery in H.D.'s garden poetry to that of her ancient predecessor is of vital importance. With H.D.'s awareness of the evolutionary process in mind, one cannot agree with Friedman's statement regarding the *Sea Garden* poems that "[t]ime exists in this realm-but not historical time" (51). It is precisely the sense of the wild, tangled view of nature so present in the *Sea Garden* poems that mark them as a production of the early modern period. While Friedman's discussion of the Hellenistic and pastoral influence in the *Sea Garden* poems is appropriate, these influences were limited by the presence of another which was potentially greater: Charles Darwin. A close examination of the evolutionary imagery in the *Sea Garden* poems reveals H.D.'s use of the ancient pastoral setting to elucidate the modern.

In *Sea Garden*, H.D.'s Imagist poems frequently involve land plants situated within seascapes as if invoking Darwin's premise that the origin of all species is the sea. One such poem is "Sea Poppies"; in the first stanza,

H.D. creates a vision of the "sea" flower which bears fruit on sand, rather than soil:

> Amber husk
> fluted with gold
> fruit on the sand
> marked with rich grain (21)

The "rich grain" is further described as

> treasure
> spilled near the shrub-pines
> to bleach on the boulders (21)

only to catch "root" by chance. The entire creation of the flower is achieved by a natural and chance process, precisely like the process of evolution.

While the poems in the *Sea Garden* evoke strong Darwinian imagery, numerous prose passages are also indicative of Darwin's influence. Lines such as "[l]ayers of life are going on all the time only sometimes we know it and most times we don't know it" (*Asphodel* 152), denote the character Hermione's awareness that she is simply a part of something which stretches far beyond the boundaries of her own existence. As she continues to contemplate the natural world, Hermione examines the human place in nature; from the excerpt below it would appear that humans are the only creatures capable of ruining nature's splendid order, while simultaneously, we are the only ones able to intellectually appreciate its grandeur:

> Colour there is in this sphere world, colour of the red sea anemone, colour as seen under clear water, colour as sea coral seen through crystal. World falls over your head and you are embedded in the world; you are its only imperfection, a fly in its clear amber; you are its only imperfections yet your very presence giving quality; point, perspective to this otherwise so measureless luminous body. (153)

The sentiments expressed by Hermione illustrate the author's awareness of the brief lifespan of humans in comparison to the timelessness of nature; when our time is ended, the "world falls over" our heads and we become "embedded in the world," fossilized like all the species which have come and gone before. H.D.'s view that humans are nature's "only imperfection" conflicts with the creationists' view of "man as the epitome of nature's handiwork" and gives voice to what Lionel Stevenson calls "Darwin's hypothesis" (5). Indeed, her language in the passage above is arrestingly like Darwin's final paragraph in *The Origin of Species*:

> Thus, from the war of nature, from famine and death, the most exalted object which we are capable of conceiving, namely, the production of the higher animals, directly follows. There is grandeur in this view of life, with its several powers, having been originally breathed by the

Creator into a few forms or into one; and that, whilst this planet has gone cycling on according to the fixed law of gravity, from so simple a beginning endless forms most beautiful and most wonderful have been, and are being evolved. (*The Origin of Species* 374)

This linguistic relationship between H.D. and Darwin should not be surprising, both for her exposure to Darwin's work as a child, and also because, according to Stevenson, as a writer and poet, H.D. should have a higher awareness of the natural world and its mechanisms. Stevenson explains that it was through poetry that Darwin's "radical implications were most fully displayed" (5) and the critic views poetic adaptation of evolutionary theory as a natural development.

For Stevenson, the natural development lies in the fact that poets, "being informed people" (15), are aware of scientific theories and their applicability. Stevenson further notes, however, that the use of evolutionary theory in poetry often takes on a metaphysical aspect. Although his discussion focuses primarily on the late-nineteenth century British poets, Stevenson's explanation seems applicable to H.D. as well. The poets were "essentially pantheists," says Stevenson, "proclaiming the progressive character of manifestation, with the quality of divine love as the self-subsisting life of the universe" (23). Stevenson sees no contradiction between evolution and universal love, and it would appear that H.D. didn't either. If we recall H.D.'s Moravian upbringing which held love to be the organizing principle of the universe, Stevenson's ideas seem increasingly indicative of H.D. The blending of evolutionism with mysticism is overt and constant in her work, a blending she shared with Havelock Ellis.

Ellis and H.D.: Womb-brains Collide

In a letter to H.D. dated July 9, 1918, Richard Aldington wrote to his estranged wife complaining to her of the "complete indifference" he had endured in the presence of former friend, Brigit Patmore (Zoolberg 101). "Brigit must now be getting into a ghastly state because of that ill-advised operation. You may remember Ellis's remarks on the matter-I think in an appendix to one of his volumes" (Zoolberg 101). While interesting for its exposure of Aldington's self-absorption (his concerns for himself are far clearer than any concerns for Patmore) and his negative view of abortion, the "ill-advised operation" responsible for Patmore's breakdown, the letter also suggests that the sexologist's ideas might be reflected in H.D. Indeed, one would expect as much, given that Ellis's theories of inversion were being widely popularized, influencing both the public perception and literary representation of lesbians and homosexuals, and as I explain below, while H.D. had not yet begun a prose text of any length, Ellis's ideas would soon erupt in her work.

As mentioned in Chapter Two, much of the fascination with Ellis in the artistic community arose from his remark in *Sexual Inversion* that "inversion is as likely to be accompanied by high intellectual ability in a woman as in a man," surprising many who had previously considered both high intellect and homosexuality to be relative anomalies in women. When Ellis commented that "[i]t has been noted of distinguished women in all ages and in all fields of activity that they have frequently displayed some masculine traits," and further that "in literature homosexuality in women has furnished a much more frequent motive to the artist than homosexuality in men" (196-98), H.D. and other lesbian or bisexual women must have been very interested. The literary texts produced by modern women frequently questioned female sexuality and lesbian relationships, as well as woman's position as artist and intellect. Ellis's work seemed to both validate and denigrate the lesbian writer. As his work also often addresses the creative center of women and its link to motherhood, there is no doubt that his texts were compelling reading for the female artistic community and society as a whole.

The modern lesbian text most notably affected by Ellis's theories was Radclyffe Hall's *The Well of Loneliness*, in which the female heroine, Stephen Gordon, nobly gives up the love of her life to the happiness which can only be found between a man and a woman. Hall, a lesbian herself, was perhaps simply catering to an audience who would accept her work only if the lesbian appeared contrite and aware of her own social position as degenerate and pariah. However, it is far more likely that Hall accepted Ellis's presentation of sexual inversion as biologically determined, and therefore, that while she was not apologetic for her sexual orientation, she was prepared to present a text in which the "genetic" lesbian ennobles herself by releasing the loving but "genetic" heterosexual woman to a more "natural" relationship. Further evidence of Hall's acceptance of Ellis's theories lies in her portrayal of inverts as "pleasant," "clever," and "artistic," all traits implicitly associated with lesbianism in *Sexual Inversion*. In the following passage from her novel, Hall describes the guests at an "invert" soiree:

> So pleasant was it to be made to feel welcome by all these clever and interesting people - and clever they were there was no denying; in Valerie's salon the percentage of brains was generally well above average. For together with those who themselves being normal, had long put intellects above bodies, were writers, painters, musicians and scholars, men and women who, *set apart from their birth*, had determined to hack out a niche in existence.

The language here is strongly evocative of Ellis's statements that "[f]eminine inversion has sometimes been regarded as a vice of modern refined civilization" *(Studies in the Psychology of Sex* 1:4 204), and the passage from Hall's book could easily be mistaken for a case history from Ellis's own work. While Hall knew that many would not approve of her book or her life, she seems to have hoped that some would recognize her slightly veiled reference to Ellis's theory and therefore view her lifestyle with his relative open-mindedness.

Indeed, Ellis's tone in *Sexual Inversion* is generally sympathetic, particularly in his introductory statements, such as:

> I found in time that several persons for whom I felt respect and admiration were the congenital subjects of this abnormality. At the same time I realized that in England, more than in any other country, the law and public opinion combine to place a heavy penal burden and a severe social stigma on the manifestations of an instinct which to those persons who possess it frequently appears natural and normal (v)

Sympathetic as Ellis was, there is little doubt that he viewed homosexuality or "sexual inversion" as a state of degeneracy, particularly when he links homosexuality with what he considers socially aberrant behavior. "The life of the prostitute may well develop such latent [degenerate] germs," states Ellis, "and so we have an undue tendency to homosexuality, just as we have it among criminals, and, to a much less extent, among persons of genius and intellect" (212). The linking of prostitution, criminality and genius with inversion must doubtless have caused great consternation among many of the female moderns; while prepared to some degree to live as outcasts from society, many modern lesbians, Hall in particular, despised debauchery and promiscuity in any form and maintained lifestyles which were extremely moderate. Their strong feelings were perhaps due to a sensitivity regarding Ellis's work.

Unlike Hall, when H.D. undertook her first novel, it was not a public apologia or explanation for her sexual orientation. Instead, H.D.'s *Paint it Today* is a more personal attempt at self-analysis and exploration; whereas Hall seemed to have but one orientation and one explanation for it, H.D. was instead, ambiguous about both her orientation and its cause. Her works are explorations of relationships, both with herself and with others; these explorations are often influenced by her reading of contemporary sexual theories.

At the center of the novels *Asphodel*, *Paint it Today*, and *HERmione* are intimate female relationships which chronicle H.D.'s sexual attraction and personal definition. Also ever-present in the texts are the men in H.D.'s life, and her relationships with them likewise had to be chronicled and negotiated as H.D. attempted to write her life. Noteworthy, however, is H.D.'s tendency to pay greater personal tribute to women than she does to men. Her lengthy articulation of love, for example, has Frances Gregg as its focus, not Pound or Aldington; to Frances H.D. directs, "I have come again away from the dead/Drawn by strange powers to thee,/Quicken me now nor fear to give,/Too much of yourself to me" (*Paint it Today* 11), her translation of Heine's poem. Like the poem, H.D.'s own declarations of love articulate a sense of spellbound fascination when the object of her affection is a woman:

> [t]he fiancé had shown Midget what love might be or become if one, in desperation, should accept the shadow of an understanding for an understanding itself. Josepha had shown her or she had shown Josepha what love was or could be or become if the earth, by some incautious legerdemain, should be swept from beneath our feet; and we were left ingratiated between the stars. (*Paint it Today* 22)

Illustrative of H.D.'s bisexuality, this passage also qualifies her lesbian emphasis, demonstrating that H.D.'s feelings run deeper for women than for men. Her sexual position therefore seems, like her nationality, to be a matter of *degree*. She is *more* lesbian than heterosexual; she is *more* European than American, but both of these aspects of identity occupy relative places on a continuum; sexuality and nationality are dynamic and seem linked to those around her, and indeed, to each other. She is American, but not so American as the "tourists"; she is in love with Ezra, but this love is only a shadow of that she has for Frances. She is aware of the depth of her feelings for Frances, but only in Europe will she openly acknowledge them. Describing their position as bisexual social outcasts, H.D. writes:

> [t]hat was natural. It was natural that she and Josepha and such as she and Josepha should be cast out of the mass of the living, out of the living body, as useless as natural wastage, excrementitious, it is true, thrown out of the mass, projected forth, crystallized out, orient pearls, to stand forever after, a reflection somehow, on the original rasped and wounded parent. (*Paint it Today* 18)

Again, however, what we term her bisexuality or bi-nationality seems more often to be really *two* sexualities or nationalities, dependant upon H.D.'s feelings *at the time*. Rather than being half-American or half-British, at different points in her life, H.D. is one or the other, never successfully "both." Like her sexuality, H.D.'s nationality shifts but does not stick; her inner conflicts, like her external geographic locations, inform who she is at different times. The continuum is controlled, seemingly, by two very oppositional points.

As she explores her sexuality and nationality, H.D.'s language in this first novel is remarkable both for its frankness and its emphatically evolutionary implications. Persistently, H.D. uses the word "natural" to describe society's exclusion of bisexuals, lesbians and homosexuals, people "such as she and Josepha." The passage above illustrates H.D.'s awareness of her failure to fulfill her natural role; while she and Gregg are beautiful "orient pearls," they do not seek to attract males and subsequently bear young. Although pearls are indeed, attractive, the use of the descriptor, "orient", seems also be a reference to Ellis's statements regarding the much higher percentage of lesbians and bisexuals in "foreign" cultures, an issue worthy of brief digression.

After explaining that in western culture far fewer women admit to inverted behavior than do men, Ellis notes that in New Zealand, Bali, and Zanzibar, inversion is "almost as common among women as among men." He further notes that "[a]lthough Oriental manners render it impossible for such women to wear men's clothes openly, they do so in private, and are recognized by other women" (*Studies in the Psychology of Sex* 1:4 206).

Like the Oriental women, H.D. and Frances do not publicly wear the male-gendered clothing associated with the female inverts Ellis describes. They do, however, "recognize" each other and find themselves "beautiful." Beautiful or not, Midget [H.D.] and Josepha [Gregg] are "natural wastage, excrementitious" because they thrive, but do not procreate. Their "unnatural" relationship is an eyesore in the natural, heterosexual world, and H.D. does not flinch from the description. Although in love with Frances Gregg, she does not hesitate to note her mother's opinion of Gregg as "an unwholesome influence" (*Paint it Today* 11). Interestingly, while the lesbian content of the passage seems clear, the final words are ambiguous, for the reader is unsure whether the "rasped and wounded parent" is society, nature, or the women's real parents.

H.D.'s feelings about her relationship with Frances Gregg are intense but complex, for even as she describes her deep love for Frances, H.D. admits to the social objections regarding homosexual relationships. Frequently, it is hard to ascertain just how much of her Moravian upbringing H.D. left behind when she came to Europe. While she could not have agreed to the degeneracy Ellis associated with inversion (as mentioned earlier), H.D. does invoke many images of Ellis, as in the passage above. Although H.D. and Frances do not wear male clothing publicly or casually, H.D. does associate boyishness or the occasional wearing of men's clothing (on stage) when writing about Frances Gregg [Fayne Rabb]. For example, in her discussion of Gregg as Pygmalion in *HERmione*, H.D. writes,

> 'Poor damn Shaw would be delighted' and Hermione hated George with his affectation of familiarity with crowned (so to speak) heads and saw that Fayne Rabb was Pygmalion. That could be no other than Fayne Rabb because ouija-board perceptions saw Pygmalion, saw a stretch of sea coast, saw a boy in a tunic who was Fayne Rabb, who was Pygmalion. (138)

The association of sea coast, of boyishness, of Pygmalion, with Fayne Rabb is evocative of the New Zealand natives Ellis described, particularly when we note that George makes no mention of Fayne's androgyny; it is instead only recognized by Hermione [H.D.].

These incorporations of Ellis's theories are evidence that while H.D. may not have accepted his association of degeneracy with inversion, she did have her own reservations about lesbianism and its social stigma; more importantly, she appreciated his discussion of the female mind and its relationship with artistic creativity, associating this with her own theory of female creativity. This latter association of artistic creativity with the female reproductive organ helps us understand H.D.'s attraction to portions of Ellis's work. His statement that "[w]omen's brains are in a certain sense . . . in their wombs" must have seemed insightful to the woman who wrote of a "womb-brain or love-brain that" she "visualized as a jelly-fish in the body." The jelly-fish or "over-mind" that H.D. refers to in the essay which comprises *Notes on Thought and Vision* is an idea which resurfaces in many of her texts. She describes the "over-mind" as a near-physical manifestation, writing that

> [w]hen a creative scientist, artist or philosopher has been for some hours or days intent on his work, his mind often takes on an almost physical character. That is, his mind becomes his real body. His over-mind becomes his brain. ("Notes on Thought and Vision" 18)

H.D. clarifies this abstract description when she explains "that overmind seems a cap, like water, transparent, fluid yet with definite body, contained in a definite space. It is like a closed sea-plant, jelly-fish or anemone" (19).

The most esoteric of her writing to see publication, *Notes on Thought and Vision* is an intense contemplation of the metaphysical aspects of creative and intellectual ability. H.D. explains these aspects as "a set of super-feelings, long, floating tentacles of the jelly-fish" which "reach out and about" (19) and these super-feelings are what make the artist "see" life with the innate ability implied earlier by Stevenson. While poets have often made references to similar "over-minds," Emerson's "oversoul," for example, H.D. is the first to insist on linking the physical and artistic creative centers in the womb.

Intrigued by Ellis's own metaphysical statements, H.D. was not content simply to read Ellis or to incorporate his ideas in her work. She also made his acquaintance, and for a time, H.D., Bryher and Ellis vacationed together in Greece; this was a strange menage, to say the least. One can only assume that while vacationing, H.D. and Ellis discussed their shared ideas regarding women's literal and figurative capacities for creation, negotiating previous notions of "cultural creation" as "an inherent property of masculinity" (Buck 41). It would seem that H.D., who "investigates maternity as a psychic state rather than a biological process" (Buck 41), would have much to say to the sexologist whose theories were continually addressing the metaphysical (*The Psychic State of Pregnancy*, for example).

Although *Notes on Thought and Vision* is the most emphatic example of the metaphysical in the H.D. oeuvre, there are numerous passages in her prose fiction which nearly equal the essays in their esoteric intensity. The metaphysical aspect of her fiction is distinctly different from the classical and natural imagery of her poetry. This is perhaps a result of the great difference in style. While H.D.'s early poems address people and events in often very guarded ways, the early prose unselfconsciously takes these events and examines their internal or psychic repercussions. The prose works also contemplate the concept of identity in far greater depth than do the poems. As H.D. explored the internal realms of her body, mind and soul, her examinations began to change from "woman as artist" to "writer and written." The subtle shift would cause H.D. to move further and further into subjectivity as she began examining and cross-examining her own psyche.

While the Imagist poems H.D. produced were "encoded" in an effort to impersonalize her poetry in keeping with the Imagist and modernist traditions, her fiction would be a radical departure into thinly veiled autobiography as she undertook herself as text, examined subjectively by herself as author. Dianne Chisholm describes H.D.'s venture into autobiographical fiction, or "lifewriting," as a gradual process which began shortly after WWI. The preliminary post-war texts H.D. created, such as *Hedylus*, were unsuccessful, "the sterile labor of an overworked and 'detached intellect'" (68). With *Paint it Today*, however, H.D.'s fictional style begins to emerge as she examines her desire for another woman. Explained by Cassandra Laity as "a modern homoerotic novel of passage," *Paint it Today* is perhaps H.D.'s most explicit female love story.

In her introduction to the novel, Laity describes *Paint it Today* as "one of three autobiographical novels (including *Asphodel* and *HERmione*) exploring H.D.'s love for women" (xvii), and which articulate "a largely biographical account in which one woman, Frances Gregg, figures as the most compelling erotic and emotional love experience of H.D.'s life, and another woman, Bryher, as her protectorate, "child," and life partner" (xvii-xviii). The novel chronicles H.D.'s relationship with Gregg in all its erotic intensity and confusion, as well as her failed attempt at a relationship with Ezra Pound. Fascinating in its honesty, the text of *Paint it Today* articulates H.D.'s fixation both with Gregg and with herself. The text is also remarkable for the very marked presence of Havelock Ellis.

In a passage describing the relationship between Gregg and H.D., Josepha and Midget in the text, H.D. plays on the language of Ellis's description of androgyny and inversion. "Somewhere in one of those outlying painted cities there had once been a Josepha, there had once been a Midget. What they had been, flower girls, or prostitutes, or captured slaves or page boys or young scribes, or one a scribe and one a butcher's daughter" (26). The blending of androgyny and inversion in this passage is fascinating, not simply for its relation to the work of Ellis, but also as evidence of H.D.'s awareness of identity as unstable. The paragraphs following this passage are increasingly evocative of the idea that identity is at best, a tenuous and momentary thing. "What do I sing? I don't know what I sing. What anyhow does it matter what I sing, I, a nebulous personality without a name" (26).

The nonsensical tone of this and other passages of *Paint it Today* belie the seriousness of H.D.'s presentation of identity. Even when named, she calls herself "Midget" in the novel, the image evoking something not merely small but misshapen. Perhaps because H.D.'s erotic and romantic attraction for Gregg was intense compared to Gregg's more laissez-faire affection, H.D. felt "small" and dominated by her "distorted" or perverse affection; as H.D. so markedly draws her identity, when present at all, from Gregg, *Paint it Today* becomes a poignant articulation of a woman who feels frequently invisible. It is unfortunate that the H.D. created here as insecure, intense, betrayed, "nebulous," returns in many texts. Seemingly, identity was only assured when H.D. loved and was loved. This theme recurs much later in *Bid Me to Live* when Julia, the H.D. character, aware of husband Rafe's (Aldington's) infidelities, becomes so depressed that her identity is reduced to the "all of me in the manuscript which you [Rafe] didn't even trouble to write me about" (*Bid Me to Live* 77). The H.D. here is so small, her identity can be hidden within the binding of a manuscript.

The disappearance of H.D. as a person here, as elsewhere, is tightly linked to the disappearance of love from her most intimate relationships. This loss of identity closely corresponds to what Hemingway seemed to experience first when he lost Agnes von Kurowsky and then Hadley (even though the latter was a loss he orchestrated himself). Both authors responded to the loss of love by seeking out both a new love-object and a new identity, linking this behavior pattern to its very Freudian beginnings in the break with their parents mentioned in an earlier chapter.

Conversely, the creation and recreation of H.D. first as poet and then novelist, is also a response to love and its loss. Weaving herself and her texts from the fabric that comprised her emotional life, H.D. attempted to make sense of the "weave" of this fabric by incorporating into her texts the theoretical explanations provided by Darwin, Ellis, and Freud. Both she and Hemingway seemed incomplete, spending their lives seeking someone or something that would make them whole. Although never completely satisfied with their lives and loves, the fragmented selves which comprised Hemingway and H.D. are emblematic of the modern experience they chronicled.

Conclusion:
"The Sea in Being"

Throughout this study, I have argued for the persistent presence of contemporary sexual theories in the works of H.D. and Hemingway and have illustrated this argument through the biographical and thematic similarities these authors share, as well as the texts they both read. I have also presented discussions on numerous works by Hemingway and H.D. which have as their most persistent theoretical symbol, the sea. As site of birth, change, transformation, and often, dysfunction, the sea as metaphor and descriptor for life dominates the works. The sea is the background for H.D.'s first collections of poems, *Sea Garden*, just as it is in a great deal of *Paint it Today*, *Asphodel*, and numerous other works. Each time one of H.D.'s characters sets off on a sea journey, her identity becomes as fluid as the water beneath her. Similarly, Hemingway uses the sea in countless stories and novels, particularly in "The Sea Change," "On the Quai at Smyrna," and *The Garden of Eden*.

The land surrounding the sea in the works of these authors is often reflective of Darwin's metaphor of the "tangled bank, clothed with many plants of many kinds" (*The Origin of Species* 372), peopled as it is with members of various communities, classes, orientations, and affiliations. The texts of Hemingway and H.D. are rich with varied "species;" their characters are often hybrids, sexual hermaphrodites, androgynes, bisexuals, evidence that nature's process of evolution is both quixotic and incomplete. The characters, like the authors themselves, struggle to form a stable identity in a world which seems intent on destabilizing it. Modern identity, like modern culture, was the result of a continual process of cultural transformation and social saturation. Both H.D. and Hemingway were keenly aware of this and this awareness led to the creation of complex, realistic, and changeable characters who are a combination of autobiography and theoretical interpretation.

Even as H.D. and Hemingway struggled to find meaning through the theoretical explanations of Charles Darwin, Havelock Ellis, and Sigmund Freud, so too did they seek to find explanations for themselves as sexual beings. Both authors struggled to understand the complexity of human sexual orientation, and even while Hemingway's view of homosexuality was predominantly negative, he often displayed a desire to understand the motivation or origin of homosexuality in an effort to shed some of the fear he so closely associated with it.

Sexually ambiguous, H.D. was never completely sure of her ultimate orientation, if indeed, such a thing exists. Her own explanation for her identity was as an "evolutionary process," and the term was one she seemed to apply to life and writing, as well. Her identity as daughter, as mother, as writer, and as woman, all underwent transformations which seemingly never ended. Even very late in life, H.D. was exploring new art forms (film) and new relationships. In both her texts and her relationships, H.D. would often embody the woman Alicia Ostriker states has

> had to state her self-definition in code form, disguising passion as piety, rebellion as obedience. Dickenson's "Tell all the Truth but tell it slant" speaks for writers who in every century have been inhibited both by economic dependence and by the knowledge that true writer signifies assertion while true woman signifies submission. ("The Thieves of Language" 315)

Interestingly, while these two writers seemed to have so much in common, their personalities could not have been more different. Reticent, elitist, and reclusive, H.D.'s personality was a distinct departure from the self-disclosing prose she would write and rewrite for most of her life. Hemingway was her opposite. Gregarious, opinionated, seemingly unconscious of class, Hemingway's most constant "haunt" was a bar. He conversed at length, wrote letters to everyone he met, and socialized regularly until just before his death. Strangely, his prose would be clean and unemotional, all digressions and unnecessary words weeded out until the text reflected only the essentials.

I have attempted with this study to open up new discussion on the modern canon, in the hopes that other scholars will acknowledge the relevance of evolutionary and sexual theories in American literary studies and may be inspired to attempt such evolutionary studies themselves. While many of the theories we use to "read" literature are extremely useful tools, I have found none which more helpfully explain the motivations behind human behavior and the creation of character in the modern era. Although all the moderns most certainly did not read sexual theories as did Hemingway and H.D., they did live and write in the era most crucially impacted by them. Just as the post-modern era would have the knowledge of nuclear power as its leit-motif, the modern era cannot be read without an awareness of Charles Darwin and the sexologists who followed him.

His *Origin of Species* and *The Descent of Man* would provide fallout just as great and far-reaching; once these works were published, the world, and the literature describing it, would never be the same.

Bibliography

Allen, Grant. *The Story of the Plants*. London: George Newnes, Ltd., 1903.

Baker, Carlos. *Ernest Hemingway: A Life Story*. New York: Charles Scribner's Sons, 1969.

———. *Ernest Hemingway: Selected Letters, 1917-1961*. New York: Scribner's, 1981.

———. *Hemingway: The Writer as Artist*. Princeton: Princeton University Press, 1963.

Beer, Gillian. *Darwin's Plots: Evolutionary Narrative in Darwin, George Eliot, and Nineteenth-Century Fiction*. London: Routledge & Kegan Paul, 1983.

Bender, Bert. *The Descent of Love*. Philadelphia: University of Pennsylvania Press, 1996.

Benstock, Shari. "Expatriate Sapphic Modernism: Entering Literary History." In *Lesbian Texts and Contexts: Radical Revisions*. Karla Jay, ed. New York: New York University press, 1990.

———. *Women of the Left Bank*. Austin: University of Texas Press, 1986.

Blau DuPlessis, Rachel. *The Career of That Struggle*. Brighton: The Harvester Press, 1986.

Buck, Claire. *H.D. and Freud: Bisexuality and a Feminine Discourse*. New York: Harvester Wheatsheaf, 1991.

Burnett, Gary. *H.D. Between Image and Epic: The Mysteries of Her Poetics*. Ann Arbor: UMI Research Press, 1990.

Chisholm, Dianne. *H.D.'s Freudian Poetics: Psychoanalysis in Translation*. Ithaca: Cornell University Press, 1992.

Comley, Nancy and Robert Scholes. *Hemingway's Genders*

Cooper, Stephen. *The Politics of Ernest Hemingway*. Ann Arbor: University of Michigan Research Press, 1987.

Darwin, Charles. *The Origin of Species By Means of Natural Selection and The Descent of Man and Selection in Relation to Sex*. New York: The Modern Library Compendium Volume, Random House, Inc. (undated).

De Lauretis, Teresa. *The Practice of Love: Lesbian Sexuality and Perverse Desire*. Bloomington: Indiana University Press, 1994.

D'Emilio, John and Estelle Freedman. *Intimate Matters: A History of Sexuality in America*. New York: Harper & Row, 1988.

Donaldson, Scott. *By Force of Will: The Life and Art of Ernest Hemingway*. New York: The Viking Press, 1977.

Doolittle, Hilda. *Asphodel*. Durham: Duke University Press, 1992.

———. *Bid Me to Live*. New York: The Dial Press, 1983.

———. *Hermione*. New York: New Directions Books, 1993.

———. *Paint it Today*. New York: New York University Press, 1992.

———. *Collected Poems*. New York: New Directions Books, 1983.

———. *Nights*. New York: New Directions Books, 1986.

———. *Notes on Thought and Vision*. San Francisco: City Lights Books, 1982.

Ellis, Havelock. *Studies in the Psychology of Sex*. 1897-1910. New York: Random House, 1936 2 vols.

Farwell, Marilyn. *Heterosexual Plots and Lesbian Narratives*. New York: New York University Press, 1996.

Freud, Sigmund. *The Basic Writings of Sigmund Freud*. New York: Random House, Inc., 1938.

Friedman, Susan. *Penelope's Web: Gender, Modernity, H.D.'s Fiction*. New York: Cambridge University Press, 1990.

———. *Psyche Reborn: The Emergence of H.D.* Bloomington: Indiana University Press, 1981.

Gergen, Kenneth. *The Saturated Self: Dilemmas of Identity in Contemporary Life*. New York: Basic Books, 1991.

Gibbons, Tom. *Rooms in the Darwin Hotel*. Nedlands: The University of Western Australia Press, 1973.

Guest, Barbara. *Herself Defined: The Poet and Her World*. New York: Doubleday & Company, Inc., 1984.

Hemingway, Ernest. *A Farewell to Arms*. New York: Charles Scribner's Sons, 1968.

———. *A Moveable Feast*. New York: Charles Scribner's Sons, 1964.

———. *For Whom the Bell Tolls*. New York: Charles Scribner's Sons, 1968.

———. *The Garden of Eden*, ed. Tom Jenks. New York: Simon and Schuster, Inc., 1996.

———. *The Complete Short Stories*. New York: Charles Scribner's Sons, 1987.

———. *The Sun Also Rises*. New York: Charles Scribner's Sons, 1968.

Hollenberg, Donna. *The Poetics of Childbirth and Creativity*. Boston: Northeastern University Press, 1991.

Lynn, Kenneth. *Hemingway*. Cambridge: Harvard University Press, 1995.

Norris, Margot. *Beasts of the Modern Imagination: Darwin, Nietzche, Kafka, Ernst, & Lawrence*. Baltimore: Johns Hopkins University Press, 1985.

Ostriker, Alicia. "The Thieves of Language: Women Poets and Revisionist Mythmaking." In *Feminist Criticism: Essays on Women's Literary Theory*. Elaine Showalter, ed. New York: Pantheon Books, 1985.

Reynolds, Michael. *Hemingway's Reading: An Inventory*. New Jersey: University of Princeton Press, 1981.

Ritvo, Lucille. *Darwin's Influence on Freud: A Tale of Two Sciences*. New Haven, Conn.: Yale University Press, 1990.

Robinson, Janice. *H.D.: The Life and Work of an American Poet*. Boston: Houghton Mifflin, 1982.

Ruland, Richard and Malcolm Bradbury. *From Puritanism to Postmodernism: A History of American Literature*. New York: Viking, 1991.

Sedgwick, Eve. *Epistemology of the Closet*. Berkeley: University of California Press, 1990.

Silverstein, Louis. "Herself Delineated: Chronological Highlights of H.D." In *Signets*. Susan Friedman, Rachel Blau DuPlessis, eds. Madison: The University of Wisconsin Press, 1990.

Spilka, Mark. *Hemingway's Quarrel With Androgyny*. Lincoln: University of Nebraska Press, 1983.

Stein, Gertrude. *Everybody's Autobiography*. New York: Random House, 1937.

Stevenson, Lionel. *Darwin Among the Poets*. Chicago: University of Chicago Press, 1932.

Sulloway, Frank. *Freud: Biologist of the Mind*. New York: Basic Books, 1994.

Wagner-Martin, Linda. *The Modern American Novel: 1914-1945*. Boston: Twayne Publishers, 1990.

Yeazell, Ruth. *Sex, Politics, and Science in the Nineteenth-Century Novel.* Baltimore: The Johns Hopkins University Press, 1986.

Yukman, Lydia. "Loving Dora: Rereading Freud Through H.D.'s Her." In *RePresenting Bisexualities: Subjects and Cultures of Fluid Desire.* Donald Hall, Maria Pramaggiore, eds. New York: New York University Press, 1996.

Zilboorg, Caroline. *Richard Aldington & H.D.: The Early Years in Letters.* Bloomington: Indiana University Press, 1992.

Index

A

Adams, Nick, 20, 21, 45, 46
African stories, 68, 77
Aldington, Richard, 11, 38, 39, 40, 52, 85, 87, 92
Allen, Grant, 10
Ames (in *Sister Carrie*), 4
Anderson, Sherwood, 52
androgyny, xxv, xxvi, 22, 26, 59, 61–65, 69, 70, 73, 76, 77, 89, 91, 93
Ashley, Brett (in *The Sun Also Rises*), xxvi, 49, 59, 62, 76
Ashton, Julia (in *Bid Me to Live*), xxvi, xxxi, 38, 92
Ashton, Rafe, 92

B

Barkley, Catherine (in *A Farewell to Arms*), 48
Barnes, Djuna, 40
Barnes, Jake (in *The Sun Also Rises*), xxvi, xxxi, 49
bisexuality, xxi, 15–17, 40, 43, 61, 71, 76, 86, 88, 93
bleaching/blonde, 63–64, 69
Bourne, Catherine (in *The Garden of Eden*), 59–68, 73
Bourne, David (in *The Garden of Eden*), 51, 62–68, 77
Bryher (Winnifred Ellerman), xxxii, 11, 17, 37, 40, 52, 90, 91

C

capitalism, 2
Christianity, 19, 73
city, 1

D

Darwin, Charles, xvii–xx, xxii–xxvii, xxxi, 2–5, 7–10, 16–17, 22, 26, 40–41, 46–48, 53–54, 56, 60–62, 72–73, 77, 80–85, 92–94
  Descent of Man, xvii, 47, 62, 82, 94
  "kill and eat," xviii
  Origin of Species, xvii, 8, 82, 84, 93–94
  sexual selection, xviii, 3–5, 53–54, 60, 62, 72
  "social Darwinism," 6, 8
  "struggle for existence," xvii, 46–48
dialogue, 69–72
de Gourmont, Remy, 39–41
domesticity, 35

Doolittle, Charles, 10, 11, 37
Doolittle, Helen, 10, 23, 35
Doolittle, Hilda (H.D.), xvii–xviii, xix–xxii, xxiv–xxxii, 3, 7–18, 23–24, 26–43, 46, 49, 51–52, 79–81, 83–94
    Asphodel, 32, 37–38, 84, 87, 91, 93
    Bid Me to Live, xxi, xxiv, xxvi, 38–39, 92
    "Griffin of Temple Bar, The," xxviii
    "Hermes of the Ways," 13
    HERmione, xxi, 36–37, 84, 87, 89, 91
    "Iphigenia at Aulis," 12
    Kora and Ka, xxi
    "Lady Leicester," xxviii
    "Mid-day," 13
    Notes on Thoughts and Vision, xxxi–xxxii, 31, 36, 90
    Paint it Today, xxi, xxviii, 30, 32, 34, 37–38, 41, 87–89, 91–93
    "Pear Tree," 13
    "Priapus," 13
    Sea Garden, The, xxi, 15, 31, 83, 84, 93
    "Sea Poppies," 83
Dreiser, Theodore, 2–4
Drouet (in *Sister Carrie*), 3

E

Ellerman, Winnifred (Bryher), xxxii, 11, 17, 37, 40, 52, 90, 91
Ellis, Havelock, xvii, xix–xx, xxii–xxv, xxvii, xxxi–xxxii, 7–8, 17, 33, 37–38, 41–43, 51, 53–54, 56, 59–60, 65–68, 72–74, 77, 80, 82, 85–86, 89–92, 94
    Dance of Life, The, xxi, 53
    Erotic Symbolism, xxi, 60, 63, 65, 68, 74, 77
    Sexual Inversion, 17, 85–86
    transcendental qualities of sex, xxi, 9, 60, 66, 68, 90
emasculation, 20, 22, 25, 61, 64
erotic imagery, 14
expatriation, xxiii–xxiv, 29–30, 37–38, 56

F

female narrative view/female gaze, xxviii–xxix, xxxiii, 80
fetishism, xxiii, 60, 62, 65, 73, 74
Fitzgerald, F. Scott, 75, 77
Freud, Sigmund, xix–xx, xxii, xxiv–xxv, 5, 7–8, 11–17, 21–22, 34, 41–43, 49–50, 55–56, 60, 66, 75–77, 80–82, 92, 94
    arrested development, 11
    castration complex, 25, 48, 63
    mother complex, xx, 11–12, 15, 27
    narcissism, 66
    Oedipal conflict, 20, 25
    penis envy, 15
    sexual fixation/obsession, xix, 8, 16, 61–62, 64–66, 68, 73–74
    sexual object selection, xx
    sexual symbols, 75
    transference, 74

G

garden imagery, 10, 14–16
Gart, Hermione (in *HERmione* and *Asphodel*), xix, 32
gender, xxix–xxxi, 14, 24, 26, 60, 73, 77, 79
Gregg, Frances, 11–12, 14, 29–31, 33–34, 38, 41, 49, 87–89, 91–92

H

hair, 26, 53, 63, 64, 69
Hall, Radclyffe, 86–87
"Helen myth," 36
Hemingway, Clarence, 19, 21, 24, 26–27, 75, 77

Index

Hemingway, Ernest, xvii–xxii, xxiv, xxvi–xxviii, xxx–xxxii, 3, 5, 6–8, 12, 19–28, 43, 45–57, 59–70, 72–77, 79, 92–94
   A Farewell to Arms, xxiv, 46, 48
   A Moveable Feast, 52, 54
   "A Way You'll Never Be," 45
   "Big Two Hearted River," 51
   "Cat in the Rain," 68
   "The Doctor and the Doctor's Wife," 20
   For Whom the Bell Tolls, xxi, 59
   "Hills Like White Elephants," 68
   Garden of Eden, The, xxi, xxiv, xxxi, 23, 51, 59, 60–61, 64, 66, 74–75, 77–78, 93
   "Indian Camp," 20
   "The Last Good Country," 22
   Old Man and the Sea, The, 73
   "On the Quai at Smyrna," 47–48, 93
   "The Three Day Blow," 53
   "The Sea Change," xxi, 68–69, 71, 93
   "Soldier's Home," 50–52, 77
   Sun Also Rises, The xix, xxi, xxvi, 49, 59, 72, 76
   "Up in Michigan," 51, 53–54
Hemingway, Grace Hall, 19, 21, 24, 26–27, 49, 51–52, 61, 63, 72–74, 77
Henry, Frederick (in *A Farewell to Arms*), 46, 48
homophobia, 55, 76–77
homosexuality, xix, xxiv–xxv, 17, 24–25, 37, 42, 54–55, 61, 63, 71–72, 75–77, 80, 85–89, 94
"homosexual panic," 76
Hurstwood (in *Sister Carrie*), 3–5

I

identity, xxi–xxiv, 27, 37, 42, 46, 49, 60, 64, 67, 79, 88, 91–94
Imagism, xxviii, xxx, 40, 91
immigration, 8
incest, 22, 34
infidelity, 40, 92
inversion, 17, 33, 37–38, 41, 61, 85–87, 89

J

Josepha (in *Paint it Today*), xix, 33, 88–89, 91

K

Krebs (in "Soldier's Home), 50–51
Kurowsky, Agnes, xxvi, 48–49, 92

L

Lake Walloon, 19, 22–23, 25
latency, 25, 75, 87
lesbianism, 33, 37–38, 40, 42, 55, 67, 70, 75, 80, 86, 88–89
London, 32–34, 36, 38

M

Mac Almon, Robert, 52
Maria (in *For Whom the Bell Tolls*), 62
masculinity, 19, 24, 27, 61–65, 69, 74, 76
matricide, 34–36
Midget (in *Paint it Today*), xix, 32, 34, 51, 88–89, 91–92
mirror imagery, 74
morality, 6, 47
Moravian, 9, 39, 85, 89
mother/child, xix, 10, 27, 36–37, 50–52, 61, 86

N

nationality, 32, 43, 46, 53, 56, 88

P

Paris, 31, 39, 40, 52–53, 69, 76
patriotism, 46–47
Perdita, 40
perversion, 42, 66, 70–71
Pfeiffer, Pauline, 65, 73
phallus, xxv, 13

Pilar (in *For Whom the Bell Tolls*), 59, 62
Pound, Ezra, 12–14, 29–34, 38–41, 52, 54, 74, 87–88, 91
prayer, 23

R

Rabb, Fayne, xix, (in *Hermione*), 32, 89
Richardson, Hadley, 52–56, 75, 92

S

"sewing basket," 10, 17
sexuality, xix, xxii–xxiv, xxvii, xxxi, 3–6, 9, 16, 26, 30, 32, 37, 39–43, 48, 50, 53–56, 59–62, 65–68, 73, 75, 78, 80, 87–88, 93–94
  ambivalence/ambiguity, xxv, xxxi, 30, 34, 38, 41, 60, 61, 94
  dysfunction, xxvi, 48, 60–61
  inversion, 17
  transcendental qualities, xxi, 9, 60, 66, 68, 75
Sister Carrie, 2–6
"social Darwinism," 6, 8
spirituality, 9, 13
Stein, Gertrude, xxiii, xxxii, 37, 40, 52, 54–55, 76
suicide, 3, 20, 21, 77

T

transgender, 64–65
"tumescence," xix
twinning, 26, 37, 62–64

U

urbanization, 1

V

vice, 71

W

war, xxiv, xxvii, 46–50, 53, 56, 91
  wounds, xxvi, 45, 49
"womb-brain," 36, 85, 90
writing, xxvii, xxxi–xxxii, 7, 14, 27, 34–36, 38, 40, 50, 56, 67–68, 79–80, 91, 94
"writing cure," xxv, 55

For Product Safety Concerns and Information please contact our EU
representative GPSR@taylorandfrancis.com
Taylor & Francis Verlag GmbH, Kaufingerstraße 24, 80331 München, Germany

www.ingramcontent.com/pod-product-compliance
Lightning Source LLC
Chambersburg PA
CBHW052131300426
44116CB00010B/1854